WEALTH
WON'T WAIT!

ESCAPE THE 9-5, REGAIN YOUR
FREEDOM, AND LIVE IN ABUNDANCE

WEALTH WON'T WAIT!

HOW TO CREATE INCOME CERTAINTY IN UNCERTAIN TIMES!

MIKE DESORMEAUX

Visit our website at www.wealthwontwait.com

First Edition: 2020

ISBN 978-1-7773931-0-6

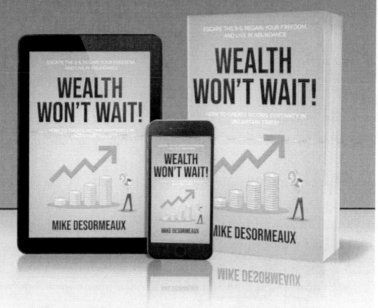

ACKNOWLEDGEMENTS

This book is dedicated to the hundreds of investors I've had the honor to work with over the past 15+ years. Without all of you, the learning process would have been much slower, and I wouldn't have so many great stories to share. I am glad we crossed paths.

To Tom and Nick Karadza of Rock Star Real Estate, who gave me a chance when I knocked on their brokerage door one fateful morning and asked if they had a position for me. They didn't, but they made one.

I am especially honored that I can call many of you friends. Here's to continuing our journey to make life better for ourselves, our families, our kids, our investors, and everyone around us.

CONTENTS

CHAPTER 5   120

Coming Up with The Money To Purchase an Investment Property   120

CHAPTER 6   128

The Five Biggest Mistakes a New Investor Can Make and How to Avoid Them   128

Preface

Everything you are doing and not doing today is creating your future.

Never before has the divide between the wealthy, middle class, and poor been as large as it is today. And the divide is growing. There are more middle-class people today who are moving towards poverty than are getting closer to being wealthy. Entrepreneurs, business owners, and investors are the people that are getting wealthier and wealthier. Employees, the people working for money, are able to afford less and less as the cost of living continues to rise. The average person's wage is not sufficient to keep up with these rising costs. Never has the cost of living and housing prices been so disproportionately high when compared to what people are earning from their job(s).

I am just an average person who helps other average people get unstuck. Real estate just happens to be the easiest way that I have seen for the average person, just like myself, to create true wealth.

I've spent more than 20 years of my life personally investing in real estate and have helped thousands of investors do the same thing across Southern Ontario. In that time, I've helped investors purchase and sell over $300 million in real estate. I've spent over 55,440 hours of my life specifically focusing on, teaching, and working in the trenches, negotiating real estate investment deals. I am confident you will be hard pressed to find another person in Canada so deeply involved in investment real estate in Southern Ontario.

I want to share this information that has helped me and thousands of others over many years.

The intent of this book is to provide you with real-life, relevant strategies for investing in real estate. There's so much content out there that sounds great in books, forums, seminars, and on social media, but those strategies often tend to be either impossible in our marketplace or incredibly difficult to implement. I'm talking about the get-rich-quick schemes, the no-money-down promises, the sandwich lease options and other 'ideas' that sound great but stop at that.

That is not this book! The content I present here is relevant and immediately applicable regardless of the market we are in.

The best strategy for anything you want to learn, whether it is investing in real estate, losing weight, gaining muscle, or playing an instrument, is to find someone who is already getting the results you want and then tap into their knowledge. This is what this book will do for you.

Whether you are a newbie or an experienced investor with several properties under your belt looking to take your investment portfolio to the next level, someone has already paved the road ahead of you. There's no need to start from scratch. There are people ahead of you who have already made the mistakes and learned from them. You don't need to make them too. When investing in real estate, an investor wants to mitigate risk as best as possible. A mistake in real estate can cost a person tens of thousands, if not hundreds of thousands of dollars and many nights of restless sleep. I've seen this happen! I hope you use the strategies in this book to avoid as many mistakes as possible and be successful in your real estate investing!

If after reading this book, you decide you are in the market for a real estate investment opportunity, contact me. You can meet with me to discuss your real estate investment goals and figure out what type of investment and return is best for you.

If at any point in this book you feel:

- You have question
- You don't understand a particular topic
- You need further explanation

- You've read enough and want to get started in real estate investing

Please feel free to reach out to me.

Email: mike@wealthwontwait.com

Follow us on Instagram @mdsoldit

Visit our website: www.wealthwontwait.com

and www.mdsoldit.com

Introduction

We Are Drowning In Noise And Starving For Wisdom

Everyone has a story

I was born in the 70s and raised as an only child. My mom had me when she was only 19 years old. I have great parents. They did the best they could with what they knew, which is very little when you are 19 years of age. I remember living in several apartments with my parents growing up. We eventually moved up and my parents saved everything they had so that we could move into a house in the West End of Toronto. The property was literally a few doors down from the Canada Packers slaughterhouses. Depending on which way the wind was blowing, you could often smell the cattle, chickens, and whatever other animals were being slaughtered.

My dad worked in factories for most of his life, and my mom pretty much did the same, along with some retail work. I remember my parents bouncing around a lot from job to job.

There were many things we didn't have, but I wouldn't say we were poor. Food and mortgage payments took precedence over car and house insurance for us back then, so having our house broken into one day was not ideal. Besides the fact that all the furnishings were tipped over and rummaged through, our dresser drawers and nightstands tossed, any little meaningful items we were able to attain over the years was taken away from us that day. I definitely attained my street smarts growing up in that neighbourhood.

As a young child, I witnessed a drive-by shooting on that very street. It was a summer night, and we had no AC in our home, not even a portable window unit. My bedroom window was open. It was around midnight when I heard a car coming down the street and then stop. I looked out my second-floor bedroom window and saw the driver of a blue Pontiac Firefly, left hand holding the steering wheel while his right hand reached across his body. He rested his right wrist on his left forearm and pulled the trigger of a semi-automatic gun while punching the gas pedal with his foot and quickly accelerating the car down our street.

Not seeing me, he was shooting in my direction into the homes and cars on the street as he drove past. I stared out the window, seeing shot after shot. Thinking back, I don't know if I was in shock or what. I don't know why I didn't duck for cover. Maybe it was because my bedroom was on the second floor that I felt out of harm's way, because he seemed to be firing straight and not aiming the gun upwards as he pulled the trigger. This wasn't a targeted shooting; it was just some random guy firing the bullets of a gun into homes and cars on our street.

I had friends who were not so lucky. One, I will use his initials, PC, was called over to a car while walking with his girlfriend to the CNE (Canadian National Exhibition). It was a planned shooting. PC was shot once in the chest and died on the scene while his girlfriend screamed in horror. Another friend apparently got into an altercation with the wrong person and was stabbed to death in a nearby laneway, where he passed. Others succumbed to drugs, and a few sped up their time on this earth by taking their own lives.

In this neighbourhood, I saw many gang fights. The image of a stabbing victim's bloody handprint on a wall is forever stamped into my memory. Back in the day, if cattle were to escape from the stock yards, police would shoot them dead in the streets while us kids would watch. This sounds like a different country, not the West End of Toronto. But it was.

In the 1980s, crack cocaine was rampant in our community. I saw too many people fall victim to that addiction. I remember seeing an addict smoking crack from a pop can that she had made into a makeshift crack pipe. She said to me, "Don't you ever try this, never try this!" It was a moment that I will never forget. Hearing this from an addict while she was getting her fix, with her knowing that she shouldn't be doing it, scared the heck out of me. I think this is why I have never tried any sort of illegal drugs.

A lot has changed since that time. The old West End neighbourhood is not the same. The slaughterhouses are all but gone, replaced by subdivisions of townhomes and large retail stores.

My parents, not post-secondary graduates themselves, never seemed to be big advocates for education. I can't say they guided me toward education or a career, however, I truly feel they taught me the most important things in life; be kind, work hard, don't complain, and be the best you can be at whatever you choose to do. The values my parents taught me did more for me in life than any education ever did.

It's our outlook and our decisions, not our story or our conditions, that determine how we will live our lives. We know there are people born with genetic advantages, financial advantages, and environmental advantages. However, we also know and hear about people who, without these advantages, have far surpassed what many people expected of them.

The turning point

Around the age of 30 I made a decision that would forever change my life and the life of those closest to me. In a few short years, I was able to go from having pretty much zero investments and no path in life to owning several rental properties in several cities across Southern Ontario.

You see, I didn't know 'wealthy' people growing up. Funny story, when I was around 10 years of age, on Halloween, a buddy of mine suggested we no longer trick or treat in our neighbourhood. He suggested we take the subway and a bus to one of the wealthiest neighbourhoods in Toronto and knock on those doors for candy. That suggestion was brilliant. Not only did we get more candies knocking on these doors, but the candies seemed to be bigger as well. This was literally my first taste of what wealth had to offer.

Into my early 20s, I still didn't know any 'wealthy' people, but I would often hear of how these people obtained their wealth. I quickly realized that the common denominator was either that 'these wealthy people' owned a very successful business, or they owned real estate. Later in life I find out that successful business owners more often than not also have a substantial portfolio of investment real estate. The stories of how these people became wealthy differed—a hard-working mechanic who once leased his garage to eventually purchase and own it; later purchasing other commercial units and then leasing those units to tenants of his own. A salesperson or blue-collar worker who worked hard and then started purchasing rental properties on the side—the common denominator was always there: the 'wealthy' owned real estate.

Realizing the 'wealthy' owned real estate, I purchased my first property in Oakville in my early 30s, got hooked, and never looked back. Today, I have helped and continue to help over a thousand investors purchase investment real estate that helped change their lives and their families' lives for the better. I have had the unique opportunity to meet and guide a huge variety of people from all walks of life: factory workers, engineers, salespeople, doctors, CEOs and presidents of Fortune 500 companies, accountants, financial advisors, contractors, new immigrants, first responders, flippers, professional athletes, other Realtors, Olympians, new and experienced investors and many other great people whom I have been blessed to cross paths with.

In the following pages you will not only read about my experience but that of hundreds of other investors whom I have worked with for the past 15+ years of my life as I continue my ongoing quest of investing in real estate and helping others do the same.

I am your road map, your compass, your GPS, or whatever the newest technology is that will get your where you want to go. I have navigated these roads before you, and I have a very well-worn path you can follow. I can save you years of pain and stress, help prevent you from losing money, and keep you from making unwise decisions.

The most expensive currency in the world is experience. There is no shortcut for experience. You can't fake it, you can't buy it, and it won't come overnight. Expertise in a specific field is becoming rarer and rarer. There is so much noise and information out there. Everyone has an opinion. Listening to an uninformed person is worse than having no answer at all. We all need to make sure to seek those who have informed answers to the questions we have. Opinions are a dime a dozen, and everyone has them. We must not mistake opinions for facts.

Malcolm Gladwell coined the term the '10,000-hour rule', referring to the principle that 10,000 hours of deliberate practice are needed to become world-class at anything. My team and I specialize in investment real estate every single day. I have been focused on this niche market in real estate for over 55,440 hours in my career. I've helped guide thousands of average people, many of whom have become multimillion-dollar real estate investors, by sharing the knowledge I have accumulated over the past 15+ years of investing in properties.

Today, I am a loving father to two wonderful boys, married to the woman of my dreams, and live in Oakville, Ontario. I continue to invest in real estate and coach thousands of investors on how to do the same across Southern Ontario.

Through real estate investing, my family and I have been able to design our lives rather than having our lives designed for us. Not only have I been able to create a great life for my wife and children and thousands of other investors, I am also looking to do the same for my children's children and for you, if you let me.

I fully understand that to share my experience, knowledge, and stories with the industry is only asking for competition. But I just felt I needed to share, as there is too much noise out there, too many opinions, courses that cost tens of thousands of dollars (completely unnecessary), get-rich-quick offers, US opportunities being pitched, and a bunch of other smoke and mirror offerings about investing in real estate that just don't sit well with me. If I can help cut through that noise and provide real, tested, tried-and-true advice, then I have hopefully made a positive, impactful difference in people's lives and set them on the right path.

That is enough about me. This book is about you and how I can help you achieve your dreams. This is the real deal, real world, in the trenches, real estate investing book by a Canadian for Canadians.

This book is about helping you to not make the same mistakes I have made or seen others make. I know where a lot of the potholes are in the road of real estate investing, and I want to share those with you so you don't have to discover them for yourself.

I truly believe that deep down everyone is good by nature. Everyone is just trying to get ahead. You are just trying to make a better life for yourself and your family. Nowadays, most people trying to get ahead will recklessly throw their money into a stock, mutual fund, or the newest trend. These types of investments more often than not do not lead to true wealth. I've met thousands of successful people in my lifetime. I am sure they are out there, but I have yet to meet an individual personally who has made a fortune by investing in mutual funds or the stock market. Cash, cash flow (like from properties), and strong assets (like properties) are very important and our safety net in uncertain times like the present moment.

You owe it to yourself to make this life the best possible life you can. You are the beneficiary of the survival of your ancestors. That's right, if you are reading this book right now, every single one of your ancestors survived and did not succumb to war, disease, natural disasters, accidents, or famine, and escaped natural predators throughout the past 200,000 years, before passing on their DNA to you. The odds of this happening are incredible. Think about what it took for you to get here, to be alive! We owe it to ourselves and to our ancestors, our families, and our loved ones to live our best lives and help others do the same. The 'problems' we have today pale in comparison to the life-or-death issues our ancestors lived through.

Our team

After reading this book you will know a lot more about investing than many people who get paid or earn commissions from providing investment advice. If you are local to Southern Ontario and want further assistance in your real estate investment career, we are here to help. Our brokerage, Rock Star Real Estate Inc., is located in Oakville, Ontario. We specifically focus on working with individuals who want to better their lives through owning investment properties. We literally handhold investors through the entire investment process, from the very first meeting. We go through the whole investment real estate process with them: getting to know their short-term objectives and long-term goals, then selecting the right type of property in the right area, advertising the property, filling the property, managing the property, and everything and anything in between.

We go well beyond facilitating real estate transactions and have an entire system dedicated to maximizing value for real estate investors. We have helped changed people's lives by providing our clients with an unparalleled prospective on investment real estate within Southern Ontario. Included in these transactions are single-family homes, property conversions, second suites, rent to owns, flips, student rentals, multi-residential, lot severances and custom builds, commercial properties, and land acquisition.

One of the biggest keys to successful real estate investing is your network, and we have that! Whom you know and who knows you goes a long way in this business.

Our inner network for real estate takes care of it all:

- A real estate team to help find and source investment opportunities

- Platinum access to the largest selection of homes for sale not yet listed to the public and not available to other Realtors

- Customized investment analysis of properties

- Mortgage brokers and financing

- Property management

- Accountants

- Architects

- Lawyers and paralegals

- Home inspectors

- Contractors and handymen

- Insurers

- Stagers

Our goal is to help the people we work with create and preserve wealth by providing the best real estate investment search/sales, financing, education, construction, legal, and advisory services available. Our job doesn't stop when we help an investor find and purchase a property. That's when our job begins. Many of the investors we work with individually own 10, 15, 20+ investment properties that we found and helped them purchase.

I wish I could tell you there is a shortcut to financial freedom and that that shortcut is super easy. Well, that type of shortcut doesn't exist, at least not legally. This book is about rolling up your sleeves and learning about real estate investing and financial freedom. In it, I will share with you how I have helped many average, regular people become multi-millionaire real estate investors. This is not a get-rich-quick scheme. The strategies you will learn in the following chapters took time; decades of work on both my team and the investors' part.

These investors are people just like you and I, who dreamed of getting out of the rat race and becoming successful real estate investors, enabling them to fulfill their individual goals, support their families, travel the world, retire, quit their jobs, start their own businesses, buy their dream homes and cars, take several vacations per year, and so on.

I don't believe I could be doing anything more exciting than what I do today. I consider myself lucky. Not only am I in control of my future, I also get to work with hundreds of incredible people (investors). Investing in real estate seems to attract people who are motivated to have more and do more for themselves and others.

I am not special! You are not special! Was that too soon? Someone had it just as bad (or worse) as you and made it. They are living the type of life filled with abundance that we all want. I am not just referring to financial abundance. They also have strong and healthy relationships with friends and family, they are healthy, they are great moms and dads to their children, they take dream vacations, they give back to their community, and so much more.

All great returns in life, whether in health, wealth, weight loss, relationships, knowledge, or success, don't come over night. They come from compound interest. Incremental, often unnoticeable progress, day after day. Look, we all want the quick fix. We are all impatient. We live in an on-demand society. From TV, to ordering on Amazon, UberEATS, Spotify; at a moment's notice we can choose what we want to eat, hear, see, read, and buy. To look 10 years ahead from now may seem like forever. Those next 10 years are going to come, whether you like it or not. The question is, "Where will you be in 10 years' time, and what will your life look like?"

Finally, I wish to thank you from the bottom of my heart for exchanging your hard-earned money and invaluable time for this book. May you learn and prosper!

CHAPTER 1

Take Control of Your Life

Life is too short to chase unicorns!

How would you feel if you knew in your mind, heart, and soul that you were financially abundant and that you and your family would not have to worry about finances for the rest of your life?

Although this book is written to describe the various ways to successfully invest in real estate; money—profit, cash flow, equity, wealth, whatever name we choose—money in and of itself is not the end goal of this venture. The by-product of investing in real estate is far more valuable than just making a lot of money. It's about making a lot out of life. It's about freedom and doing what you want, when you want. It's about freedom of choices and freedom of time and creating income certainty in uncertain times.

There's hardly ever a week that goes by that I don't meet someone who tells me they want to invest in real estate. They often have a job that they hate; involving long hours, pressure, and a lot of stress, whatever their profession. These burdens too often lead to these people hating life and/or worse, bringing home their frustrations to their spouse, kids, or family if they are still lucky enough to have one. This is a numb and unpleasant way to go through life and completely unfair. These are good people trading their limited time on this earth for money, and more often than not they may also be struggling to stay ahead and get out of debt.

If you are working eight hours a day and then include travel time to and from work, that is the largest portion of your waking day spent on one thing—work. This doesn't include the additional time required if you have the type of job where you have to work at home and/or on

14

weekends as well. I meet too many people who work more than eight-hour workdays, putting in 10, 12, 14-hour days at a minimum of five days a week.

The modern workforce is burning the candle at both ends, and people are desperately seeking the ever-elusive work-life balance. We're all looking for a way to slow down and enjoy life among all of our responsibilities. Yet how can we slow down and even attempt a greater work-life balance if we have to provide for ourselves and our families? Don't get me wrong, I am not a pessimist. But these are stories and complaints that I hear from people on a weekly basis. It seems too many people walk around in life as if they are serving a prison sentence even though that prison is unguarded and all doors are unlocked.

Where will you be 10 years from now?

Where were you 10 years ago? Where were you mentally? Physically? Were you single? Dating? Married? Where did you think you would be today? Are you there yet? Have you achieved your hopes and dreams? Now that you have thought about your past, where do you think you will you be in 10 years' time? It is going to flash by you like that! The next 10 years is going to happen and there is nothing you or I can do about it. The question is who will you become? What will you have accomplished, contributed and achieved when you get there?

You may be one of the fortunate ones who currently has a job making six figures and would be considered 'well to do' by many. However, anything can happen to bring a sudden end to your income. Your company could get sold or downsized, competitors could take over the market, the company or product could become obsolete, or you could get ill or injured. These things can happen to anyone, whether you're a business owner, employee, or a professional athlete.

Let's say everything plays out well. Are you, right now, perhaps in your 40s or 50s? If you are, how many years do you have left with your company? Maybe 10 years left? What if you are forced out of that company? How easy will it be for a person in their 50s or 60s to find another well-paying job? Companies want longevity and sustainability. They are less likely to hire and train someone who only has a few working years left in them versus a much younger person who will be with the company for years and work their way up the corporate ladder. We live in a world where individuals, couples, and families are all working more than ever, yet have less and less to show for it. We are also living longer, often well into our 80s and 90s, but we can't work forever. What will life look like for you when you retire?

Covid-19

I started writing this book months prior to the Covid-19 pandemic, at a time when the world seemed to be moving along quite normally. Kids were in school, parents were working, families enjoying dinners out, fans were cheering on their professional sport teams, kids were playing in parks, there were gatherings for weddings and birthdays parties, people travelled for vacations on planes, trains, and cruise ships, and stadiums were packed for concerts. We are presently in the Spring of 2020. All of this has come to a grinding halt, along with the world's economy. Everything has been forced to close. Our children cannot go to school. Retail stores and malls are closed. Stadiums, churches, recreation centers, parks, theatres, and restaurants are all empty, seven days a week, 24 hours a day. The entire world's population is living under some type of stay-at-home order. Everyone's lives have been impacted by this disease. The outbreak is moving quickly, and the governmental responses and outlooks change day by day. Some countries seem to be at the peak of infection, while in other countries cases are rising rapidly. Some are experiencing a resurgence from their initial wave of infections. Social distancing is our new norm for now. For those fortunate enough to be healthy and able, when they do travel outside for necessities, they usually don't go closer than six feet from others and often wear protective gloves and masks to avoid infection and transmission. Businesses are losing revenue, because the government has forced all non-essential businesses to close. Companies have laid off millions of workers just in Canada alone. Hundreds of businesses are filing for bankruptcy to never reopen. Nobody knows what our new future will look like. Usually we can extrapolate from past patterns to help us with a general expectation of what the future will look like. The problem we are facing here is that there is no past history for what we are engaged in to learn from. We are simultaneously faced with the worst public health crisis in recent times, the worst economy since The Great Depression, the worst collapse in oil in history, and the greatest stimulus program from central banks and governments around the world. These are four unique circumstances that we're encountering all at the same time, and our future has never been so blurry. The tragedy left behind from the path of this virus is yet to be seen, but it will be like absolutely nothing we have seen in our lifetime. We are facing the prospect of a deep and lasting global recession, regardless of the health and economic policy measures taken by countries around the world. What is clear is that the impact on humans is already tragic, both health-wise and financially. At the same time, we have never felt so close as a community. The entire world is suffering from this pandemic together. Everyone is going through the exact same thing at the exact same time with the exact same ultimate consequences if this virus infects us; life or death. If there is ever to be a time when people come together on this planet, the time is now, and I think we are capable of doing that. The people that survive this are going to understand what it means to go through adversity as an entire planet.

I can't shed light on how long all this will last; it's impossible. And I hate saying this, but unfortunately it is the reality: There has never been a better time to have cash, cash flow, and assets. The world is literally in hysteria right now, and despite government assistance, no one is going to provide for you or your family better than you can. Let this be a wakeup call to us! The 9 am to 5 pm rat-race job that the majority of society adheres to is not going to cut it. Whether you own a business or work for someone else, that single income is fragile, and there is no backup if that is all you have as a source of income in your life. Once we get through this pandemic; if you are not already financially free, if you don't already have investment assets or a successful business, the majority of you are going to pay a major price, and your children are going to pay an even greater price if you are not able to provide them with a good financial foundation to start from. I hope that after you read this book you will further realize, more than ever, how important it is to have multiple streams of income to support you, your family, and loved ones. You will not only be able to take care of yourself and loved ones, but you will also leave a legacy to be remembered by.

Presently, we don't know if we are in the thick of Covid-19 or still in the beginning. The 'flattening of the curve' hasn't happened yet. No one is sure what the final outcome will be. One thing is for sure though—this will pass. But it will leave behind massive, massive destruction. Too many people will die after succumbing to the virus. Others will struggle to pay bills and catch up on the debt they piled up while they couldn't work. Many will be unemployed, looking for work on a planet where millions of businesses will no longer be hiring because they were forced to close their doors forever. Other businesses simply won't rehire because they need to cut costs in this new economy.

Whenever we get to what our new 'normal' will be, I think many people will be awoken. I know I am guilty, and I think many of us are, of walking around taking our vulnerability for granted. We can't fear what we can't control. However, we must grab a handle on what we can control, and that is our financial responsibility and ultimately our freedom. As we cope during these times, people will become more aware than ever where the gaps in their lives are, be it financial, health, relationship, career or investments. The most obvious hole will be seen financially for those forced out of work and business. Never has income-producing assets been as valuable before. They can better carry us through this pandemic and through the new 'normal' that lies ahead of us.

Money

People with money have problems, and people without money have problems as well. I've had no money and problems in the past, and let me tell you, when you have money it's a little easier to take care of your problems.

Money also provides a lot of mental real estate in your brain. Once you have the basic necessities covered—food, shelter, security for you and your family—you don't have to waste mental energy on stressing about upcoming bills or "can we really take that vacation we want to take, or can we really afford this or that?"

Getting out of the rat race and acquiring true wealth involves owning assets, such as investment real estate or a business that will generate income for you. These assets will require you to invest your time, but the time you invest in real estate and the financial returns you make on that time is disproportionate to what a good paying job pays you. Proper assets can make you hundreds of thousands to several millions of dollars over time, with really not that much time invested. How long would you need to work to make a million dollars? How about a couple million dollars?

For most hardworking people, a good portion, if not all, of the money they work for goes to support themselves or their family and their current lifestyle. What if you could financially support your lifestyle but then had another million or millions made for you by your assets that you really didn't have to work that much for? That's an extra million or two to play with. These sound like big numbers, but they are really not. It just takes time. It's not get-rich-quick, I don't have that magic pill; it's get-rich-slow. But time flies!

Most people want out of their 9 to 5. I get it. Building a real estate portfolio will be their biggest asset that will provide them with the ability to do so eventually. Most of the successful real estate investors that I work with take this approach: They continue with their 9 to 5 jobs while they expand their real estate portfolio. Then they leave their jobs to move on to bigger and better things once they can replace their job's income with enough cash flow from their rental properties. After these investors quit their 9 to 5, they tend to either replace their new free time with being full-time investors. They might start a property management company and help others to manage their properties or start a new business that they always wanted to start but couldn't because they were chained down to their former 9 to 5 and simply didn't have the time. Others who enjoy their 9 to 5 or are business owners might choose to keep working for a certain amount of time but have much less stress knowing they've substantially increased their additional income and would be ok if they were to lose their current employment income.

I don't know how old you are, but I will assume you are in your mid 30s to late 40s. Once you pass 40, time goes by very quickly. Believe me, 50 will come in a blink of an eye. I am almost 50 as I write this. Whether you're 30, 40, or 50 now, life is going to fly past you, especially your productive years. If you are not financially stable now and don't have the wealth you want in your life now, for you and your family, let's getting going! We don't have time to waste.

The system is rigged against us!

The government, the man, the system, whatever you label it, has us living in a world where governments and banks constantly devalue currencies with low interest rates and print stimulus money, flushing trillions of dollars into the economy. This is a time like never before where you want more assets, not less. Everyone living in Southern Ontario who have not held real estate over the last 10 to 40 years are being hit with a wealth transfer that they don't even know about. The dollars in their bank accounts have less and less buying power as essentials like food and shelter continue to become more and more expensive.

Imagine you are a parent with a piggy bank full of coins. You also have a couple of toddlers. Each day these toddlers take a couple of coins out. The coins only come out two or three at a time. You don't even notice that the coins are diminishing. Your savings, the coins in your piggy bank, in our analogy, are able to purchase less and less. Some of us might be ok with our toddlers taking our money, but I don't think anyone would be happy with the government taking money from them.

We are literally being robbed by the government and central banks without even noticing it. They are devaluing our savings and the money we work hard for with stimulus money. Holders and savers of money are getting left behind more than ever. So, how do we protect ourselves? If you can afford it, you buy assets. You should, of course, also save dollars for a rainy day, but you should get the rest of your money out of savings and into good assets. Money saved is buying us less and less day by day, and we need to get that money into good assets that will be worth more than the money we put into it over time. Too many people dabble in investments for their financial future, and they pay an enormous price for it. It's not because these people are not smart or they don't care, but is often because of their inexperience and insufficient comprehension of investments like the regular go-tos stocks and mutual funds. They are too busy to research and partake in other options. Mutual funds are lazy investments with high hidden fees, and I proudly own none! There are high frequency trading machines far smarter than any human trading stocks. There are also some of the smartest minds in the world working for big companies trading stocks. Someone has to lose in order for another to profit. I don't feel confident gambling my hard-earned money against a computer or playing against some of the smartest stock traders in the world. There are much better ways to invest money and actually come out ahead. The most common investment assets that I have seen people purchase and achieve great financial wealth with is by far investment properties.

You need the right mindset

You have to have the right mindset to be successful in real estate. If you think that those who are wealthy are undeserving or lucky, you are distancing yourself from success. I don't believe you are that type of person, because you chose to read this book to better your life, therefore you are probably not the type to expect things to be handed to you. I don't believe people can just earn their way to financial freedom from a job. Besides, the government will make sure you only receive 50% of that hard-earned income that your employer paid you. You need to invest, successfully, to achieve freedom. We are finite life forms and we shouldn't be doing something we hate every day. It's time to see how we can break free and live life on our terms.

CHAPTER 2

What Investing in Real Estate Can Do for You

Years tell what the days can't show!

Take responsibility

When it comes to the areas of our lives that matter the most—our families, our health, our faith, our finances—we can't rely on others guiding us on what to do and then unquestioningly follow that advice. We need to take responsibility and take care of ourselves. We need to ask ourselves questions, get answers, and make smart decisions. I refuse to give someone else control of my and my family's finances. I am 100% in charge of my own investments, and that's the way I want it. I've given up my most valuable asset, 'time', in exchange for income—income that I use to invest. I will never get back the time that I exchanged for income, so I want to treat that money with the utmost respect.

How much monthly income do you want?

How much monthly cash flow would you like from real estate? Is it an additional $5,000 or $10,000 per month? Is it just enough cash flow to replace your current income, allowing you to get out of your job? How many properties would you like? What would you like your net worth to be in 10 years' time? 1 million? 5 million? 10 million?

Investment real estate is literally the best business in a box

It's no surprise that we feel investing in real estate is one of the, if not the, best businesses in the world. As a real estate owner, your business success is not affected by your age, education, looks, race, colour, or how good or poor of a salesperson you are. You have something that absolutely everyone needs: shelter.

In the business of real estate, your tenants are your customers , and they will pay you regularly for years and even decades to come. Income from real estate—rent—tends to go up in value over time. Even though property prices can go up and down in value, prices mostly go up over time. Having a good home in a good area is your key to success here.

Each month, you earn cash flow and you gain equity as you pay off the mortgage debt. There are many tax advantages. You can pull tens of thousands to hundreds of thousands of dollars out of that business if needed by refinancing, getting a home equity line of credit, or selling one of your properties. And most importantly, it's a business that you can easily pass down to your children to run, forever the bearers of good fortune from your work.

All investing is not the same

All investing is not the same. If you get a 5% return on stocks or mutual funds and a 5% return on real estate, you don't end up with the same profit; it's not even close. Since 1970, properties have appreciated at an average of 6% year over year across Southern Ontario, despite appreciation going up and down. Now, talk to a financial advisor or someone behind a bank counter, and they're probably going to tell you that stocks have done the same, so, "Why don't you just invest your money in stocks or mutual funds?" They may go on to say that it's the same return and "safer!", when in fact the exact opposite is true.

A 5% increase on your stock or mutual fund is not the same as a 5% return on an investment property. What makes investing in real estate so powerful is leverage. If you have a total of $50,000 to invest, you either saved up $50,000, or maybe you borrowed the $50,000 from a home equity line of credit. If you put that $50,000 into a stock or mutual fund and that investment increases in value by 5%, you will have made $2,500 after a year.

However, if you take that same $50,000 and use that as a down payment to purchase a property for $500,000, (assuming a 10% down payment), you now own a $500,000 property with your $50,000 investment. If the property appreciates 5%, the same appreciation as our stock example, that increase of 5% is on the overall value of $500,000, not 5% on the initial $50,000 deposit. It's all about the leverage.

Don't be afraid of the math; if you take a moment to understand the math it will set you free. Stay with me here, as this is such an important point. Your investment in real estate, with the same appreciation of 5%, with the same amount of money, $50,000, didn't make you $2,500 at the end of the year, it made you $25,000. You made 5% on the appreciation of $500,000.

To explain it another way: You would have had to invest $500,000 with a 5% return in the stock market or mutual fund to make the same $25,000 that you would make by investing $50,000 by buying a rental property in our example.

It gets even crazier if you extend the forecast to 10 years down the road. First, I will compare stocks and mutual funds. Say you got really lucky, and despite all the hidden fees in mutual funds and turmoil in the stock market, somehow you are the greatest stock and mutual fund investor in the world and you have made 5% year over year for 10 years in a row. This means that in 10 years, your total investment will have profited you $31,444 ($50,000 with a 5% return compounded over 10 years). Compare that to a rental property that you held on to for the same amount of time—10 years. At an appreciation rate of 5% per year, (historically below the average appreciation rate for Southern Ontario, by the way), a $500,000 property with appreciation of 5% compounded over 10 years will now be worth $814,447, translating to a net gain of $314,447 on your same $50,000 investment. That sounds great, right? You can take $50,000 and put it in stock or mutual funds making 5% and at the end of 10 years turn that into $31,447, or you can purchase a property and potentially turn that into $314,447.

Am I not forgetting something, you might ask? What about the monthly cash flow that you will have been getting from your rental property over 10 years? Let's say the monthly cash flow is only an extra $200 per month after all expenses. $200 x 10 years or 120 months is another $24,000 in profit.

What about the principle that was paid down on the mortgage from the rental income? After 10 years of making mortgage payments, the rent you have collected has decreased the mortgage loan by roughly $148,000. So, in total, on your $50,000 invested in real estate, you made $486,447 after 10 years, not $31,444 like in our mutual fund/stocks example. Better yet, what if you had two rental properties? Two properties x $486,447 equity = $972,894, or three properties = $1,459,341 in equity…catch my drift?

Let's say property prices flatline for the duration of the standard mortgage period of 25 years. So, for 25 years, property prices have remained the same and didn't go up. This has never happened in our lifetime, by the way, but let's assume for some strange reason it does happen. Even though you only invested $50,000 to purchase a $500,000 property, after 25 years, the mortgage on your property would be paid off in full thanks to your rental income, and you would own the property free and clear. You made $500,000 on a $50,000 investment over 25 years on mortgage pay down alone. In this example, the return is 900% (or 9.65% annually), which is still very profitable even in a very unlikely scenario. I will just leave this information with you and ask, where do you think property prices will be over the next 25 years across Southern Ontario—higher or lower?

It takes time to build something of value

Unfortunately, there's no quick way to build true wealth and abundance consistently without putting in the time to do the work and doing that work intelligently. It takes time to build anything of value. Investors that look long-term have very little competition, and that's because so many people are running around looking for shortcuts to real estate success and wealth. When you play the long game, there is very little competition. Just know that the vast majority of people are running around looking for the easy route to success; the new flash in the pan get-rich-quick idea, and that means there is less competition for you.

What real estate has done for investors

Like any business, there is work involved in real estate investing, and there will be many unpleasant days. However, the amount of time you have to invest in real estate and the return of income on that time far exceeds the income one makes from working a regular, even successful job.

I've seen investors like Dan and Laura, one being a paramedic the other a truck driver, take their dream vacation and travel for three months through Australia and Switzerland with two toddlers, able to do so from the income from their rental properties. Without those properties, they wouldn't have been able to afford the time nor have the money to take such a dream vacation.

Below are some of the most common goals that investors I work with have achieved:

- Quit their jobs after they had enough monthly cash flow to replace the income they were earning from their job or business

- Buy their dream cottage

- Be able to assist with the down payments for their son and daughter's first home

- Quit their job and start their own online business

- Do the renovation on their home that they always wanted

- Take their dream vacations

- Install the pool they always wanted

- Purchase their dream car or motorcycle

- Pay for their child's education

- Help support parents or a family member in need

- Give back to their family or favorite charity

- Get braces for themselves or someone in their family

- Purchase their dream second home in Costa Rica, Florida, Alabama, Arizona, etc.

- Pay for specialized medical treatment offered in another country to help a loved one

- Earn themselves the freedom and security of knowing they don't have to be worried about losing a job or becoming ill or retiring without being able to support and enjoy their lifestyle.

All those dreams and desires were achieved through courage and action. We all know someone who constantly complains about their current situation, whether it be relationship, finances, friends, their job, or something else, and it is often because they are not doing anything to better their situation. Inaction comes at a cost, especially when it comes to money and wealth creation. Unless you intelligently get your money working for you, the cost of not doing this can be financial, emotional, or physical. Ultimately, it can cost you your freedom. Don't let inaction cost you!

CHAPTER 3

Far Fewer Canadians Are Going To Be Homeowners

Don't wait for tough times to make smart decisions!

Increasing property prices, increasing student loans, strict bank lending, immigration, and supply constraints, both legislative and natural restrictions and policies, are the major reasons renters and those presently living at home with their parents will be staying where they arc for a while longer (if you are a parent, presently with a teen at home, right now you may have cringed). Demand for rental properties is higher than we have ever seen it, and it will continue to grow. Let's take a look at some of the key reasons why the rental demand is so strong and growing in Southern Ontario.

Property prices vs. income

The real estate market has its ups and downs. Real estate prices are pretty much like spinning a yo-yo up and down while walking up a flight of stairs. Prices will go up and prices will go down, but over time, the market will grow steadily. On average, homes in Southern Ontario have gone up 6% year over year since 1970. Meanwhile, the average Canadian's income has gone up only 2.5% during that same period of time. The difference between 2.5% income growth and 6% real estate price growth is a big deal. Real estate prices have consistently outpaced income growth. From 1970 to today, the average income has increased by a factor of seven, while real estate prices across Southern Ontario have increased by a factor of 30.

The brutal reality is that income has not and cannot keep up with property prices, and affordability is going out the window for homeowners across Southern Ontario.

Increasing student debt

I personally have a love-hate relationship with this one. I believe going to university or college can 'help' by giving us a slight competitive advantage in life. I'm not saying everyone should do it or needs to do it, not at all. I know people who have done really well in their lives and careers without having had any form of post-secondary education. But formal post-secondary education is definitely needed for some professions and specialties. I don't think I would want a surgeon working on me if they didn't graduate from a post-secondary institution! At the bare minimum, I feel most people who have gone through college or university learn 'soft skills' such as improved writing and communication, dealing with deadlines, research, problem-solving and just working well with others. You don't have to go through college or university to get those skills, but there's a good chance one will be more competent in those areas if they do.

But I also feel there is a major drawback to attending college or university. Colleges and universities are big business, and business is booming. Back in 1994, tuition was a little over $2,000 per year. Now, in 2020, it costs over $6,500 per year, an increase of 225%. Textbooks have followed this pattern as well. Now, has the quality of education really risen 225% between 1994 and 2020? I feel there is an argument to be had against the rising costs of tuition and books.

Students often leave post-secondary schools with massive debts, anywhere between $30,000 to $150,000, depending on what they studied and whether they lived on or off campus. These graduates, now in the workforce, will be paying back that $30,000 to $150,000 loan plus an additional 28% to 100% in interest. That's an additional $8,400 to $150,000 on top of their initial loan, depending on how fast they can pay it back.

How is it so ridiculously easy for a student, someone who is 18 or 19 years of age, to get a loan from the government for $30,000 to $150,000 but impossible for them to go to the bank and try and get a regular loan of even $5,000?

Student debt is one of the leading factors preventing Canadians from having children or buying a house at a younger age. It has a cascading effect, meaning that more and more young Canadians will be in the rental pool longer than they have ever been in the past. They simply can't afford nor qualify for a house as easily as others have done before them.

Immigration

The rate of population growth around Southern Ontario has not been normal for years. I am not aware of any other city on this planet that has experienced and is experiencing the rate of population growth that we are. Although Canada has a lower population number than California and slightly more people than Texas, Canada receives more immigrants per capita than the entire U.S. We're an incredibly diverse, desirable country to come to, and we a have pretty open immigration policy. On top of hundreds of thousands of people immigrating into Canada every year, there is literally no real reason for Canadians who are already here to leave Canada. We are one of the most peaceful, welcoming countries in the world. We have an abundance of quality, diverse employment opportunities, clean cities, free health care, and one of the top educational systems in the world. Is there a better place on earth than Canada to live and raise children?

Southern Ontario's population grows by over a 100,000 new immigrants per year. That's the equivalent of a new Hamilton added to Southern Ontario every five years—and that is a very conservative estimate. Canada's government's projection is for three million more people to enter the Greater Toronto Area by year 2040. Meaning that's literally another population the size of the City of Toronto headed our way to Southern Ontario within the next 20 years.

The world's largest greenbelt

Ontario's Greenbelt is the world's largest greenbelt. It circles the Great Golden Horseshoe covering the area of the Oak Ridges Moraine and the Niagara Escarpment. That's Niagara Falls to Cobourg, over 250 km around the Greater Golden Horseshoe, and consists of two million acres of protected land. The Greenbelt, brought into effect by legislation passed by the Government of Ontario in 2005, is there to preserve and protect the natural environment: farmland, forests, wetlands, rivers, and lakes, while helping the fight against climate change and putting a limit on development. The legislation that surrounds it limits where we can build and how we will develop and expand as a region to deal with our growing population. It will continue to impact us as we run out of developable land. The Greenbelt is fundamentally needed to filter and replenish groundwater. It also reduces our flood risks and provides home for wildlife. Farmland makes up 40% of the protected Greenbelt, making it essential to sustain a reliable source of local food for the region.

Not only would it be political suicide for someone in our government to open up the Greenbelt to development, but the cost of infrastructure to support new communities would just be too expensive. We would have to build sewers, roads, and sidewalks. Utilities such as gas, water, and electricity would need to be supplied to these undeveloped areas. You'd need schools, recreation centers, transit, and everything else that make up a community's infrastructure. That money will have to come from somewhere, and tax dollars will not be enough. This is why intensification targets have been increased in Ontario, demanding that builders build high-density communities like condos and stacked towns, often mixed with retail and commercial spaces to reduce the environmental blueprint and integrate with preexisting infrastructure in developed areas. This is why we no longer see detached homes being built on large lots in Southern Ontario. With Lake Ontario on one side and the Greenbelt on the other, we are literally like a little island in the grand scheme of things. Soon there will be nowhere to build, just up!

If you are already a homeowner, this restrained growth is one of the major reasons you are the beneficiary of rising appreciation of your home. It's not that your physical property costs more, it is that the land your property is on is worth more. This is the result of some simple but often overlooked fundamentals—supply and demand. We have a high demand for housing but not enough land to build on. Considering the growing population and the lack of land to build housing on, there's a massive housing crisis headed our way. Throw in the fact that we have the largest demographic coming down the pipeline (millennials) needing housing but who can't qualify to purchase a home…these key indicators alone show why it makes sense to own income-producing hard assets like rental properties. Those that own properties are going to benefit the most from these fundamental constraints individuals face when living in Southern Ontario.

CHAPTER 4

What Type Of Property Should I Buy?

It is better to miss a good one than buy a bad one!

What are your short-term objectives and your long-term goals?

"What type of investment property should I buy?" is one of the most common questions I am asked by investors when we first meet. They want to know—should they purchase a single-family home, multi-residential property, student rental, rent-to-own, do a conversion like a second suite, flip, commercial plaza, storage facilities, land-and-build, or buy a preconstruction house or condo?

The question is a loaded one. Before answering that question we need to determine what the investor's short-term objectives and long-term goals are. Knowing this is essential in order to properly build the right foundation and building blocks to the investor's overall long-term success. Not determining this upfront can lead to a haphazard portfolio of investment properties. They might still be profitable, but if we had a proper investment plan laid out from day one we could possibly do much better.

If positive cash flow is the short-term objective, that will take us down a particular path of choices of the types of properties and the areas to invest in. Positive cash flow real estate can be attained quite often by purchasing a legal two-unit dwelling, rent-to-own, a smaller multi-residential building, student rental, or converting a single-family home into multiple units. These types of properties can potentially produce positive monthly cash flow anywhere between $500 to $1,900 per month, per property, after all expenses.

Some investors' short-term objective is not immediate cash flow but rather ease of investment and management. Often, this type of investor is earning a solid income with their current employer and/or business, and they are looking more for ease of management and equity paydown on the property. Immediate cash flow is not important for them at this time. This objective might lead us into the single-family home category, which is the easiest type of investment property to purchase and manage. These properties can be easily found and purchased and can be absolutely turnkey. An investor can close on a good home, in a good area, with no updating of the home required. With single-family homes there's only one unit to fill—the home— and one family to collect cheques and take any calls from. The property can also easily be placed into property management so that this type of investment becomes 100% turnkey. Very little time investment is needed for this type of property, which makes single-family home investing one of the most popular types of real estate investing vehicles across Southern Ontario.

Another person's short-term objective could be to build up equity or scale as quickly as possible. This can involve the 'BRRRR strategy' (buy, rehab, rent, refinance, repeat), which we discuss in Chapter 4 or maybe it involves flipping a few properties, making a profit on each one, building up a nest egg, to then later purchase multiple buy-and-hold properties once enough profit has been attained through flipping.

We also need to take into consideration the investor's long-term goals before determining what the best investment strategy would be. No two strategies are the same. These goals can range from earning enough passive income from real estate to replacing your own or your spouse's current income so that one of you or both of you can quit your present job. The long-term goal can also be to own a specific number of properties, a plan for retirement, becoming wealthy, having some properties for your children and wealth to pass down to them, a way to supplement your own expenses, and the ability to attain financial freedom or a multitude of many other types of personal goals and desires.

During our initial meeting with investors, we figure out their short-term objectives and long-term goals together. This first meeting is usually anywhere between an hour and a half to two hours. During this meeting, we draw out a plan and come up with steps on how we are going to achieve their short-term objectives and long-term goals over the next 12 months and 2, 3, 5, 10+ years. After the meeting, we usually coordinate a time and date to do an educational tour. We jump in our cars and travel through the different cities across Southern Ontario to educate the investors on the pros and cons of each city and property as well as discussing rent numbers, cash flow, and true property values.

Time investment

How much time do you want to commit to your property? How hands-on do you want to be? These are questions we go through to determine the best investment strategy and area that is going to give you the results you want. Anyone can go out and purchase an investment property, but the key is really gaining the knowledge you need to determine what will be the best investment for you, now and in the future. Different investors have different portfolios that suit them. What may be good for one investor might not be good for another investor, because of differences in our time availability, capital or work, our age, or family commitments.

Time is our most cherished commodity. Before embarking on your real estate investment journey we have to determine how much time you want to spend on investing. Do you have minimal time, for now, and therefore need a more turnkey solution where we or a Realtor finds the property for you, fills it with a tenant, and then manages the property for you as well? We can arrange that. Do you have a little more free time than most people and want to be more hands-on? Someone with a little more time on their hands may want to join my team and I while we physically go through various investment properties across Southern Ontario on any given day. My team and I tour properties and investment opportunities with investors pretty much daily, screening and discussing what makes a good investment, what makes a bad investment, and why. We show them the different neighbourhoods, the desirability of the community, and the amenities in the area. Then we crunch the numbers to determine if any properties on the short list are worth putting an offer on and purchasing.

We have solutions for investors we work with who don't have a second to spare. Once we have our initial meeting and learn the investor's short-term objectives and long-term goals, we know what to look for. Some of our investors never even see their investment properties before they put an offer on them. They trust my team and I to reach out to them when we find a good investment property. We send them all the details on the properties; photos and spreadsheets; we share the strategy for the property, and then they purchase. One investor, who has already purchased 23 investment properties with me, purchased his last two properties while he was on the beach in Mexico. Everything was done over the phone and Internet. When I first met this investor he wanted to leave his company but was used to a certain standard of living. His high-end financial advisors were not performing for him so he couldn't just quit his job. He also didn't have the time to look at properties with me, nor did he have the time to manage his properties due to his career commitments. He desperately wanted out of his career. So, we set up a plan. After purchasing 10 properties, this investor, whom I now proudly call a friend, resigned from the successful company he was president of. He continued to purchase a total of 23 properties and today still looks for more investment opportunities and just closed on his second dream vacation home. His time now involves waking up, working out, yoga, travelling, and doing pretty much anything he desires. His success in real estate has also allowed him to come to Haiti with me, along with other investors I work with, to build homes for the less fortunate. All of this being possible from his trust in us that we would find him the right type of investment properties.

So, for those who want to invest in real estate but are presently too busy, I never want that to be an excuse. My team and I will find the property for such clients and assist by getting the property filled with tenants. We do all the screening of tenants, we write up the tenant contracts, and then we arrange to have the properties property managed. It is a 100% turnkey investment. Some investors love these deals because the investment is found for them and the property is 100% managed for them. The investor literally never needs to take call and can simply sit back watching the monthly rent cheques come in.

Location

Not only do we need to determine what types of properties are best for a particular investor at a particular point in their life, but we also have to determine where the best locations for these properties are at the time. We are incredibly fortunate to have many of the most desirable cities and towns in Canada right here next to us in Southern Ontario where we can purchase our investment properties. There are so many great places, but it is impossible to forecast that 'best' place. Looking ahead years into the future, it's impossible to forecast what type of property will appreciate best in a particular area, which is the answer most people are looking for. But we can make a very good educated projection based on the data we constantly gather—statistics from our own investment properties and the other over 1000+ investors we have worked with—the insights and connections we have with builders and developers, property management companies, contractors, and people in multiple levels at the city, town, and in government. We have our finger on the pulse of the real estate market, and we have unprecedented knowledge and a very good idea of what is happening in each of our local markets: supply and demand, rent prices, best mediums to advertise to renters, how long it takes to fill a property, vacancy rates, employment, transit, future development in the area, what type of property in what area is most desired, and more.

Some investors we work with like to invest where they live. We mainly work with investors who live anywhere from north to Barrie, east to Bellville, west to Sarnia, and south to Niagara Falls. We also work with investors that are not local and from places such as Ottawa, Windsor, and the United States who invest here in Southern Ontario as well.

When an investor decides to potentially purchase an investment property in the city or town in which they live, they are usually motivated by the idea of being close to their investment property and other times having the option, in the future, that the investor, themselves, their parents or their children could live in the property one day if they so desire. Again, this all comes back to the investor's short-term objectives and long-term goals.

Other investors are not so concerned about a particular city to invest in. I personally fall into this category. These types of investors just want a good investment in a good area. These investors have more good investment opportunities available to them and can generally scale their real estate portfolio faster since they are open to several different cities. There are simply more properties to search through if we are looking at 3,5,10 different cities versus just one city. There are always thousands of properties listed for sale across Southern Ontario on any given day, but only a handful at best would make for a good investment. Therefore, the more open an investor is to have investment properties in multiple cities, the quicker they can build and scale their portfolio of properties.

One can also have a combination of both strategies; a few properties in the city or town you live in and a few outside of your area.

Price-to-rent ratio

I grew up in Toronto and I live in Oakville. Yet, the majority of the real estate we own and help investors purchase are just outside of Toronto, around Southern Ontario. This is because a single-family home in Toronto currently costs about $1.2 million in an average neighbourhood. We could buy that same house on the Hamilton Mountain, in Cambridge, Kitchener, Barrie, Guelph, St. Catharines, Durham and other cities just outside of Toronto for $500,000 or less. That's less than half of what we would pay in Toronto for the same home. If we travel a little further out to cities like London, St. Thomas, Woodstock, Orillia, Belleville, Welland, and Niagara, we can pay even less for the same type of property. The rent we would get for the $1.2 million Toronto home would be roughly $2,800 per month. The rent we would get for the same type of property if it were on the Hamilton Mountain, Cambridge, Kitchener, or Barrie would be roughly $2,300. We paid $700,000 less for the property, and the difference in rent per month is $300. Our return on investment, our ROI, is much greater with our Hamilton Mountain, Cambridge, Kitchener, Barrie, Guelph, and St. Catharines properties versus a Toronto property. The price-to-rent ratio is much better on the outskirts of Toronto than it is in the city of Toronto. The tenants living in these homes, whether they live in Toronto or just outside of it, come from various employment backgrounds: school teachers, electricians, office workers, tech industry, retail, hospitality etc. Regardless of whether they work in Toronto or Cambridge, their salaries or wages are often the same for the same type of occupation. Someone working as a schoolteacher, a nurse, or at a Starbucks in Toronto doesn't get paid more than someone doing any of those services just outside of Toronto. So, if we purchase our properties just outside of Toronto, we tend to have tenants who have higher disposable incomes, which means the tenants in our homes can often better afford the home we have for rent, because they are spending less of their earned income on rent while usually enjoying a bigger size home than they would be renting if they lived in Toronto. Meanwhile, our Toronto property would incur negative cash flow, while our property just outside of Toronto would incur positive cash flow.

Hindsight is 20/20

Any homeowner and investor who has purchased in the Greater Toronto Area would have seen remarkable appreciation since 1970 and should be doing quite well. However, that is the benefit of hindsight. Looking back is by no means a way to predict the future. Most of these Greater Toronto Area homeowners probably purchased their homes out of necessity for themselves and their families, not for speculation. However, even the small percentage that did speculate have reaped some tremendous rewards in appreciation over the years. Although I agree that Southern Ontario has some of the strongest fundamentals to be found anywhere on this entire planet— immigration, job growth, education, healthcare, development and infrastructure, desirability—there's no doubt in my mind that we should all be prepared for anything and everything. The key is to never purchase solely relying on appreciation and over-leveraging ourselves. True wealth in real estate is built over time and not through speculation. I like good starter homes in good areas, because people always need a place to live during any economic cycle, down or up, good or bad, and this segment of the market, starter homes, although not immune to changes, should experience the least fluctuations as compared to higher priced properties. As an investor in real estate I've been through the 2008 global financial crisis, the 2017 real estate crash when the government of Canada implemented the foreign buyer tax, the provincial Fair Housing Plan setting in place stricter rent controls, and the stress test lending implemented by the federal government. Now, as I write these very words, we are on day 28 of being quarantined as a result of the Covid-19 pandemic. I predict that the luxury real estate market in Southern Ontario will be negatively impacted once again. I saw luxury homes from Toronto to Oakville fall hundreds of thousands of dollars as result of the 2008 and 2017 crises. Some people bought at the peak of the market to then sell their home and move into a new one at the bottom of the market. Houses that were selling for 1.5 million to 2 million just months prior were selling for hundreds of thousands less. But you know what homes did not drop in value during those turbulent times? Starter homes. Starter homes of $550,000 and less did not drop a single dollar. Sure, maybe there were fewer buyers and fewer multiple offers, but these properties did not lose their value. Do you know what else about these homes was not impacted? The amount these properties were getting in rent. While fewer and fewer people were looking to rent a luxury home at this time, the demand for starter home shelter did not change.

Needless to say, I don't feel it would be wise, for example, to purchase a property solely relying on appreciation. But at the same time, let's put ourselves in the best position to get it. Let's purchase where there is good job diversification, new employers setting up shop, low vacancy rates, desirable neighbourhoods, increase in population, great schools and adequate public transportation and infrastructure. Purchasing for positive cash flow will help you in a down market, because it is much easier to ride out the bad market when your bank account is still positive every month, and you can hold onto your investment until the market regains its footing again. There is no better time to say this than now. This predicament we are in now could never have been predicted, and we will never be able to predict something like this the next time around either. Our best defense is a good offense!

How I decided which investment properties to purchase

My wife and I currently have properties in seven different cities across Southern Ontario, and we continue to grow our portfolio.

I wasn't married when I started investing in real estate. I was working full time in sleep medicine at St. Mike's Hospital in Toronto, where I would assist in diagnosing sleep disorders. I always knew I wanted to have a career helping people. Throughout university my goal was to become an athletic therapist. However, while completing my last year of final exams, a position came up at St. Mike's Hospital that involved sleep medicine. I was always fascinated by sleep and still am today. I applied and was hired. My role involved treating patients from 7 pm to 7 am. My schedule was completely the opposite from most people's work schedule. I had to do these hours, because that's when people sleep.

Even back then I would always look long-term, and I knew that there was no way I could be married and raise a family successfully if I had to stick to this schedule. I was conflicted. I enjoyed helping people, however, looking long-term I didn't think the 7 pm to 7 am schedule would be appropriate to maintain a healthy family life, even though I didn't have a family yet. I totally understand that there are many people working all hours of the day and they live a very happy, fulfilling life and have a great family unit at home. I commend those people for being able to do so. Doctors, nurses, paramedics, firefighters, police, factory workers, and many others that are valuable to society and making an honest living. I personally know those hours are not easy. I'm absolutely not knocking their careers. I just felt for me, personally, those late night to early morning hours was not the type of work I could see myself doing for the next 10 to 20 years while being truly happy and fulfilled.

Another motivation to change my career was knowing that 'rich people' always own real estate. I wanted to make a better life for me and my future family, and I knew my hospital pay, no matter how many hours and days I was going to work, would not get me to where I felt I needed to be.

I decided my short-term objective was to build a portfolio of investment real estate across Southern Ontario so that I could resign from my job and become a full-time real estate investor.

My long-term goal was to have enough properties so that the cash flow and equity buildup would provide me and my future family with financial abundance to do what we want, when we want: To provide for our retirement, provide for our children's education, afford us the ability to take care of our parents, allow us to give back to our community and other important organizations that have meaning in our lives, and the ability to pass down properties and wealth to our children and grandchildren.

Once I had my short-term objectives and long-term goals decided, I had to decide how much time I wanted to invest into these objectives and goals. The time you personally put into real estate investing is the time spent looking for properties, then reviewing numbers, details, and research to determine if that particular investment makes sense. There's also the time to fill the properties with a tenant and the time required to manage the property.

I don't really find finding properties time intensive. We can literally find a good property, in a good area, to purchase within a couple of weeks. In Southern Ontario, filling a property with a tenant and managing it also doesn't require that much of a time investment, trust me. On average, we fill a property with quality tenants anywhere between the first showing and the tenth. That's after doing two showings, max, per week. On average, anywhere from five to 15 tenants will show up per showing thanks to our marketing strategies which I will share later. I once did a showing where, I swear, I had at least 30 prospective tenants at the house at one time.

Properties in Southern Ontario fill fast simply because rental demand has skyrocketed. An economically healthy city's vacancy rate is 4%; our vacancy rate around Southern Ontario is 1.5%. There are simply not enough good properties out there for renters across Southern Ontario. Buy the wrong type of property in the wrong area, then sure, it may take you much longer to fill it. But here we are talking about filling a good property in a good area.

In 2015, I witnessed a trend change that is even more significant today. I was filling a rental property for an investor in Hamilton by the GO station. We picked this property up for a little over $200,000. It was a single-family home; three beds, two baths, with a decent size backyard. Years prior when I would advertise a rental in Hamilton, mostly Hamiltonians looking to rent would come to the property. In

2015, the shift happened. Buyers were not only getting pushed out of the Greater Toronto Area because property prices were rising, but renters were also being pushed out due to a rapid increase in rent prices. On this particular day that I showed, there were couples from Waterdown, Etobicoke, and Toronto mixed in with the usual Hamiltonians. The Toronto couple was best qualified and moved into the property. Although this couple, who had two small children, worked in Toronto, they could rent a single-family home in Hamilton for less than what they would have paid to rent a two-bedroom condo in Toronto. Because of the location of the property, they could also easily walk to the GO train to get to and from Toronto for work. There is absolutely no shortgage of tenants for good properties in good areas in Southern Ontario.

Lastly, I had to consider the time required to manage the property. Living in Oakville, I knew that I wanted to be within an hour's distance drive to my rental properties and no more. This is because I planned to personally fill and manage my local properties. That left me with many great cities to invest in: Hamilton, Cambridge, Kitchener, Guelph, Stoney Creek, St. Catharines, Brantford, and other properties just outside of Toronto.

Originally, when I started to grow my real estate portfolio I had very limited funds. Therefore, I started with the rent-to-own strategy first so that I could use the tenant's option payment towards my next purchases. I did this a few times before starting to purchase buy-and-hold properties. I started with a few rent-to-owns, which quickly catapulted me to some buy-and-hold properties. From there, as equity built up, I started purchasing single-family homes and converting them into legal second suite properties to increase my monthly cash flow. I could purchase single-family homes for $400,000 and fill them as straight rentals for $1,900. But by converting them to legal second suites, I could collect a total of $3,225 per month by renting the two suites to two separate families.

Then I started purchasing student rentals to increase my monthly cash flow even further. Again, if we chose to rent these properties out as single-family homes, market rent would be around $1,900 per month plus utilities. Turning these homes into student rentals and renting by the room, I was now getting rent of $3,625 per month.

It takes time to build a real estate portfolio and goals can change over time. But if you have a general understanding of what your short-term objectives and long-term goals are, you are aligning yourself for greater investment success.

Should you manage your rental properties?

The decision to have your property managed versus managing it yourself comes down to how much time you have or want to spend on it. More often than not you will not be getting weekly or even monthly calls from tenants, unless of course you own a large apartment building. A tenant typically only calls you if something comes up, like an appliance not working, a dripping faucet, or a running toilet. Outside of easily manageable scenarios like those, you would not usually get many calls. Once your property is filled with a good tenant, you usually spend your time each month depositing the monthly rent cheques.

Most property management companies charge anywhere between 6% to 12% of gross rent for their management fee. If we take an inexpensive property management company that charges 6% gross rent for their management fee and our gross rent is $2,000 per month, that means the property management company is charging us $120 per month. Spread the property management fee of $120 over a few properties and that can quickly become $1,000 per month that you are paying a property management company to basically cash cheques. That's an extra $1,000 per month that could have gone towards your monthly cash flow.

Now don't get me wrong. Property management companies can be vital and make your life as an investor much easier. First, your schedule with your career and your family obligations may have you burning the candle at both ends, and you simply don't have another second you can squeeze out of the day to handle a rental property or take a call from a tenant. That's fine. Don't let that stop you from investing in your future by buying real estate. Property management is the way for you to go, at least until you have freed up some of your time.

My wife and I have some of our properties under property management. Considering we live in Oakville and have some student rentals in London close to the University of Western, we gladly pay a fantastic property management company that we have been working with for over a decade to manage those properties. Our general rule of thumb is that we manage our properties within a one-hour car ride or within 100 km of where we live, otherwise those properties default into property management. No ifs or buts; that's our rule.

The motivation for having our London properties under property management is twofold. First; the distance. London would eat up too much time if we were required to drive out there to tend to an issue. I, like most real estate investors, got into real estate investing to get out of the rat race and have freedom; I don't want to be bound and lose hours of the day on tending to something else, another 'job', like tending to a maintenance call for a property.

The second reason we have our London properties managed—no offense if you are in university or college—but for most of these students it's their first time away from home. They often don't have the life experiences that you and I have. A small maintenance item that should be looked after may easily be overlooked by a student and the most common type of resolution might not be that common to them. For instance, I can't tell you how many student rentals I have walked into and encountered a slow-dripping tap or a running toilet. More often than not, utilities is added onto the rent, so these students' water bill is higher than usual simply because they don't know that they should tell the landlord that there is this issue of a running toilet or dripping tap. A better story yet; I take care of the properties of some close friends of mine when they go away for a month to their summer home in Europe. They do this every single year. Once I received a call from this friend. He said that he had received an email from a York University student at one of his properties. The student had emailed him stating that there was no hot water coming out of the taps. My friends in Europe asked me to meet the serviceman at the property. I was able to get into the house using the key in the secure lockbox. A lockbox is a must-have for emergencies and should be kept in a hidden location outside the property. This is not only good for when a contractor needs to get into the house whether someone is home or not, but is also great in a scenario if a student locks themselves out in the middle of winter and can't get into the house. I entered the code on the lock box, got the key, and the serviceman and I entered the house. We went into the basement where the hot water tank was. This was a nine-bedroom student rental property. The basement unit had two bedrooms, a washroom, and second kitchen. In one of the bedrooms, adjacent to the mechanical room with the hot water tank, I saw a student talking to a friend on Skype on her computer. I had knocked on the front door of the house earlier, before using the key, and no one had answered. I thought that perhaps she hadn't heard us. I introduced us, saying that I was friends with the owners and was there with the serviceman to get the hot water working again. She said, "Ok, great! When you finish, can you please take a look at my room, I have no power!" Now, the lights in her room were off, but I could see her computer plugged into the wall. First, I thought perhaps a circuit breaker had tripped and that was why she had no lights in her room. But before I checked the panel, I decided to check the absolute most obvious option. I went to the kitchen, took out a light bulb from a kitchen light, brought that light bulb to her room and switched it for the one light bulb in her ceiling light fixture. Guess what, there was light! Or in her case, power! Crazy! She didn't know that all she had to do was replace the light bulb. Could you imagine, as an owner, if you got a call from a tenant stating I have no power and it ended up being a light bulb? Needless to say, if the property is over an hour away, and especially if it is a student rental, I am happy to pay a good property management company to manage those properties. The cash flow from student rentals is one of the highest producing cash flow properties. The $100 to $200 bucks per month for property management, when you are typically making anywhere between $600 to $1,200 in positive cash flow per month, is money well spent.

Rent-to-own properties

Rent-to-owns, sometimes called lease-to-own or lease-options, are traditional lease agreements that also give the tenant an option to purchase the rental property, most often a single-family home, from the investor. Rent-to-owns are most often viewed as a win-win for the landlord and tenants. This is a beneficial option for tenants who otherwise would not be able to qualify for and get into homeownership. It is beneficial for the investor because with the rent-to-own program, the investor receives an upfront option payment from the tenants and the monthly rent is higher than the average monthly rent for the area. There is also an appreciated predefined buyout price that is set on day one for a second- or third-year purchase. If successful, the tenant will qualify for a mortgage at any point within the two to three years and can purchase the property from the investor. The investor then usually uses the profits to go out and quickly purchase additional investment properties.

The rent-to-own strategy is a great way for an investor to leverage an option payment provided by the tenant. The investor is essentially using other people's money to purchase their next properties sooner than they would be able to if they had to come up with the down payment themselves.

Option payments

With buy-and-hold properties, tenants usually provide the first and last month's rent upfront. But with rent-to-own, tenants are providing a down payment called an option payment, which is usually anywhere between $10,000 to $20,0000 plus first and last month's rent. The option payment is non-refundable. If the tenant qualifies to purchase the home two to three years down the road, then the option payment goes towards the purchase price of the property. If the tenant happens to walk away from the home, the tenant forfeits the non-refundable option payment, whereas in the rent-to-own program, tenants do everything they can to improve their credit and qualify to purchase the property from the investor.

Over a decade of going through this process with thousands of tenants, we've seen option payments much greater than the standard of $10,000 to $20,000, such as quite a few $50,000 payments. The highest I've ever seen or heard collected was by an investor I work with, who received an $85,000 option payment. Why would a tenant pay $85,000 as an upfront, non-refundable option payment? Usually $85,000 would be enough for the 20% down payment required to qualify to purchase a starter home in Southern Ontario. This particular tenant received a large inheritance. Despite the fact that the tenant had such a large down payment, no banks would qualify the tenant for a mortgage because their income and credit score was lower than required. This particular tenant was a single mom taking care of two children and she desperately wanted to get out of the neighbourhood she was living in. She wanted to get into homeownership, and rent-to-own was her opportunity to do so.

We never want to set up a tenant for failure in the rent-to-own program, especially when they are putting up a large option payment. Whether it's a $10,000 or $85,000 option payment, we want to make this a win-win arrangement as best as we can. Before an investor collects an option payment from a prospective tenant, we have a mortgage broker run the tenant's credit and look at their ability and likelihood to qualify for a mortgage over the next two to three years. If a tenant has no chance of qualifying in the next two to three years, we do not choose that tenant for the rent-to-own program, regardless of the amount of non-refundable upfront payment the tenant is offering us. It's simply not fair to the tenant. If the tenant doesn't qualify after three years, the rent-to-own agreement expires. If the investor doesn't then extend the option agreement for the tenant, the tenant contractually forfeits the option payment.

We investors are people trying to help other people (tenants) get out of renting and into homeownership. We are not just using the rent-to-own strategy for profit; we have a moral obligation to tenants as well. If the mortgage broker, after reviewing a tenant's current credit, payment history, income and expenses, states that yes, within the next two to three years the mortgage broker or bank can get the tenant qualified for a mortgage, as long as the tenant follows the credit advice of the mortgage broker, then perfect, those are the families (tenants) we want to choose for our homes and make homeownership possible for.

Rent-to-owns can assist the investor to scale quickly

Towards the end of 2016 I met with a young couple who were newbie investors. They had enough of a down payment for one starter home investment property up to a maximum of $400,000 and no higher. They were nervous to start because this was going to be their first investment property together. They told me, with a firm demeanor, that their goal was to purchase one investment property in 2017. Knowing that they were nervous, only had enough money to purchase one property, and lived in Ancaster, I set up a plan that would focus our efforts on the growing popularity of a specific geographical area of St. Catharines. The plan for this nervous couple who wanted one property was to purchase a single-family home that they would then offer as a rent-to-own to tenants. This way, the option payment collected from the tenant could be used towards the down payment for these investors' next property, considering they only had enough for a down payment for one property. They reconfirmed with me to make sure that I understood that they only wanted one property for 2017. I assured them that I had heard them loud and clear. The plan was successful, and they closed on their first property at the beginning of 2017. Seven months later this young couple had 14 properties. Now, two years later, they have over 30 properties. What happened? They were successful with their first rent-to-own, collecting over $54,000 in an option payment from the tenant. With their second property they collected over $26,000 as an option payment. They kept using the option payments tenants were giving them as down payments on their next investment properties. When these investors ran out of down payment money to be able to purchase their next property, they started doing a combination of borrowing private money and joint ventures with other investors. This is typical with investors I work with. We often start their investment career while they are working some other full-time job. Once they get successful at investing in real estate and have enough cash flow coming in from their investment properties, they usually get their real estate license, quit their job, and pursue real estate investing fulltime. Not all people quit their jobs when doing well in real estate, but many do. It's one of the luxuries investing in real estate affords us. This young couple both left their high paying careers and are now investors full time. They have since opened up a property management company where they manage some of our investors' properties as well.

The rent-to-own agreement

The rent-to-own agreement is made up of two agreements: the regular Ontario standard lease agreement, and an option-to-purchase agreement. These two agreements must remain as two separate documents and not combined as one.

In a rent-to-own agreement, the title to the house remains in the landlord's name until the tenant exercises their option to purchase the property from the owner.

The lease agreement is typically a three-year lease, written out on the Ontario standard lease form, which is the contract between the tenant and landlord stating the amount of rent the tenant shall pay, the date the rent is due, what the rent includes, and what the rules and terms are of the rental unit. It also has a section on responsibilities of both tenants and landlords and outlines additional terms that may be included in the lease.

Just as in a regular rental agreement; in a rent-to-own agreement the tenant has the responsibility to make timely and exact payments of rent. These monthly rent payments are typically higher than they would be in a standard lease arrangement for a similar home. This is because an agreed-upon percentage of the monthly rent, usually $200 to $500 each month, is accumulated and applied toward the purchase price of the home when the tenant purchases the property from the investor at a future date. This credit accumulation literally acts as a forced savings program for the tenant that builds equity in the house throughout the duration of the rent-to-own agreement.

The option agreement provides the tenant with the exclusive right to purchase the property for a future appreciated purchase price, usually two to three years into the future. In most cases it is in the tenant's best interest to qualify and purchase the property from the owner. However, the option agreement is exactly that for the tenant—an 'option'. The tenant does not have to buy the property, whereas the seller (investor) is obligated to sell to the buyer (tenant) within the terms of the contract.

Rent-to-own is often a great strategy for an investor to get started in real estate investing if it is their very first time investing in a rental property and they're a little nervous. (Nervous of a tenant being delinquent with rent payments, nervous about repairs, or nervous about how the tenant will treat the property.) The substantial upfront, non-refundable option payment means that the tenant has much more skin in the game than when renting your home from you. Tenants who choose rent-to-own are doing everything they possibly can to qualify for a mortgage and purchase that home from the investor. The tenants often treat the home as if it is their home already, even though the investor is still on the title and owns the home. After all, the tenants' full intention is to qualify and eventually purchase the home that they are currently renting from the investor, so they treat it with extra care.

To encourage the tenant to take care of the property while they are in the rent-to-own, the option agreement has a clause in it that states that the tenant is responsible for the first $300 in repairs, and that amount resets each and every month. The reason for this clause is because with the rent-to-own, we are trying to promote homeownership. This clause helps get the tenants to proactively take care of the home that will eventually be theirs and to prevent any nuisance calls to the landlord. Tenants have told me that they appreciate this sense of responsibility and the house feels more like their own instead of having the landlord come by any time there is small issue they could have taken care of themselves.

As per the Ontario standard lease agreement, tenants in the rent-to-own program need to reach out to the owner of the home before they make any alterations and repairs to the property. With rent-to-own, I've found that about 50% of the time tenants will reach out to the investor asking if they can improve and upgrade the home by doing such things as changing the flooring, updating the kitchen or bathrooms, putting in a new backyard fence, finishing an unfinished basement, etc. This all needs to be approved by the owner first. But if done professionally, at the tenants' expense, why not let the tenants do these upgrades? They pay for it, and these upgrades stay with the house whether or not the tenants purchase the property in the end. These upgrades increase the value of the property, which would help the investor pull some equity from the house if the investor wanted to refinance and put that money towards another rental property. More importantly, the tenants get to upgrade the rental property, making it feel more like a home for their family.

I've helped investors and tenants purchase over 1,000 rent-to-own properties together across Southern Ontario. These rent-to-own properties afford tenants, and families, the opportunity of homeownership in a way that would most likely not otherwise be possible. Many tenants who choose the rent-to-own program have never owned a home. Usually, they can't qualify to purchase a home with a bank due to circumstances such as a low credit score, too much debt, not enough of a down payment, business owners who are not fully reporting their actual income, or families new to the country who haven't established credit yet. These families dream of owning their own home, yet they can't qualify to purchase a home through conventional banks. Therefore, they are left with paying their landlord rent each and every month and seeing nothing come out of it other than a roof over their head. Many of these tenants I meet flat-out tell me they have problems saving, and in our consumer-driven world, it's hard to blame them. This is what entices people who have problem saving to the rent-to-own program; it is a forced savings program for them. Their original upfront option payment and their monthly credit all get accumulated; they can't touch that savings and spend it. That lump sum will ultimately go towards their purchase price once they qualify for the mortgage and purchase the home.

The future purchase price of the home must be agreed upon by the tenant and investor at the time the rent-to-own agreement is signed. Both the landlord and especially the tenant should know everything they are signing up for. If you ever heard of a rent-to-own going bad, with a tenant stating they were ripped off or scammed, it is usually a case where the owner didn't tell the tenant upfront what the purchase price would be two to three years down the road, and they probably didn't sign a contract. Then, two to three years later when the tenant can qualify for a mortgage and purchase the home, the landlord tries gouging the tenant by asking for some outlandish amount higher than the current market price. This is why the two-and three-year buyout price must be determined and agreed upon on day one and an option agreement signed to lock in those buyout prices.

The two- and three-year sale price is usually determined by adding conservative appreciation to the property and compounding that price year over year. This appreciation number changes, of course, depending on what kind of market we are in, the type of property, and where it is located. In Southern Ontario we have seen an average appreciation of a little over 6% year over year since 1970. I see most investors appreciating properties in key areas of Southern Ontario at a minimum of 5.5% year over year. So, if a property were purchased by an investor for $450,000, the year two buyout price for a tenant would be $474,750, and the year three buyout price would be $500,861. In my 14 years of doing rent-to-owns I have never seen a tenant purchase a property for current market price at the end of the three years. Tenants have always, in my experience, been able to purchase the property for less than market value because the properties that we purchased appreciated at a rate greater than 5.5%. This means that tenants have often purchased a home for below market value. However, even if they had to pay market value, they finally achieved their dream of homeownership. The investor, on the other hand, knew what they were going to make from day one when they signed the agreement. The investor's profit is pretty much the difference between the investor's purchase price and the sale price to the tenant. The investor would also profit from the mortgage principle being paid down for three years and the monthly cash flow from the property. Most investors make, on average, anywhere between $100,000 to $150,000 on this type of investment after three years, depending on the purchase price of the property, the appreciation rate used, the interest rate, and cash flow from the property.

Are some investors not happy when the tenant purchases the property for say $550,000 but the actual market value of the home at the time of the purchase is $600,000? Yes, absolutely! But no one has a crystal ball. The investor didn't technically lose any money, they may just have left some money on the table. This is one of those glass half empty half full scenarios. The silver lining, even when an investor potentially leaves tens of thousands of dollars on the table, is that they still made what we knew they were going to make going into this type of investment, and now a family, our tenants, have achieved the dream of being proud homeowners.

Not all tenants who choose the rent-to-own program end up purchasing the property at the end of two to three years. Every tenant obviously signs up and starts with the full intent of qualifying and buying the property from the investor, but unfortunately, sometimes life happens, and the tenant has to walk away from the home. I've found that tenants who walk away from the rent-to-own and forfeit their deposit are usually dealing with something like a marital breakup or a major job loss, and they need to downsize and find more affordable accommodation until they can rebuild.

When a tenant chooses to walk away from the rent-to-own and not purchase the home, they forfeit the upfront option payment and the monthly credit. However, we sometimes give the tenants some money back to give them a little bit of a helping hand to deal with the unfortunate and unforeseen circumstance they have encountered. Sometimes the tenants are walking away from an option payment of anywhere between $10,000 to $20,000 plus all the monthly credit they may have accumulated, potentially an additional $10,000 to $20,000. It's rare, but unfortunately the tenants may be walking away from anywhere between a total of $20,000 to $50,000. Although the investor is not contractually obligated, nor would the tenants expect it, the investor can give back a portion of the option payment to the tenant if they choose to. I would recommend that this only be considered if the tenants have been good tenants and the house has been left in either very similar or a better condition than when the tenants first moved in.

I am often asked, "If a tenant walks away and leaves tens of thousands of dollars on the table, don't they trash the house?" I have never ever seen a trashed home. These tenants are usually honest, good people who chose the rent-to-own because they wanted to get into homeownership. Unfortunately, circumstances changed and they needed to walk away. In fact, why would they want to deepen their troubles by being financially responsible for 'trashing a house'? They don't need that added stress and financial hardship. The investor could sue the tenant for damage to the house and have the tenants' wages garnished until the repairs are paid off. There's also a good chance that the investors' insurance policy would cover any vandalism. So, it's obviously not in the tenant's best interest, nor would there be any motivation for them to take out their frustration on the property.

Back in the early 2000s when I was filling one of my properties as a rent-to-own, one of the couples that came to the property told me they liked the program but they felt that the property was too small for their family. They asked me if I had any other homes available. At the time, I didn't have anything else. I asked them what they were looking for and they told me they needed a larger home; four beds, two full baths, and two stories. The property they had come to view was a three-bedroom bungalow. I asked them what kind of down payment (option payment) they had, and they said they had $20,000. I asked them what they could afford per month for rent, and they said $2,500. Knowing this gave me an idea of the price of property I could purchase for them. I had the best scenario here; I had tenants whom I could purchase a home for and use their option payment towards part of the down payment to purchase a next property. All I needed to do now was find a larger home that they would be happy to own in the future. I did my due diligence to make sure we were the right fit; credit check, employment check, reference check, pay stub checks, mortgage broker qualification etc., to make sure these tenants would be able to qualify to purchase the property two to three years down the road.

After showing them a few properties listed on the market for sale, they decided on the ideal home they were looking for, located in Waterdown. They gave me the $20,000 option payment, which I then used as part of my down payment towards the purchase price of the property. This family lived in the home for a little over two years. One day I got a call from them out of the blue. They said that their two daughters had gone off to university and now the house was too big for them. Could I help them find a smaller home in the area? I think you can imagine my response. I reminded them that the main reason I bought the home they were in was because they wanted a 'bigger' home. Now I was left with a house that I wouldn't have necessarily purchased but did because that was the home they wanted.

Back in the day, this home was the highest priced property ever purchased by myself or any other investor that I worked with as a rent-to-own. Despite this fact, I felt pretty confident with this purchase because the option payment, $20,000, was a good portion of the down payment that I could use to purchase the home for them. Also, the monthly rent they agreed to pay, $2,500, more than covered the property expenses, and cash flowed quite well. Worst case scenario, if they walked away, I knew that Waterdown, a much smaller community back then in the early 2000s, was a great place to invest. It was booming with new development, new businesses, growing infrastructure, and population. I felt strongly if the tenants ever walked away from this property, I would still own a good home in a good area.

I told them I could definitely help them find a smaller home, but I couldn't use their original option payment and their accumulated monthly credit, another $8,000, towards the new home they wanted because I now had to come up with another down payment to purchase the new home they wanted. They were fine with this, as they just wanted a smaller home. Logically, it would have made more sense if they were able to get qualified for a mortgage purchase to buy the home they were in, sold that home, then downsized into the new home they now wanted. However, they still were not in the position to qualify with a bank for a mortgage to purchase the property they were in, and they were impatient. While we were looking for the new, smaller home I asked them to reach out to the mortgage broker I work with. They tried their bank and were denied, but I convinced them of the benefit a mortgage broker can often offer. Luckily, because this was a smaller home they were looking for and therefore less expensive than the home they were in, the mortgage broker was able to get them qualified for mortgage financing of this new home, and they were able to purchase the property themselves. This was ultimately the best scenario for them. In the end, they asked me if I wanted a testimonial.

I believe that they only offered to do that because they knew everything upfront about the rent-to-own program and there was nothing behind the curtains from day one. They knew they were forfeiting their option payment and credits. We always had a respectful relationship. Instead of taking them up on their offer for a testimonial, I gave them a few thousand towards the purchase of their new property. It's not something I always do if a tenant walks away from a rent-to-own, but I felt it was the right thing to do with this particular family.

Another example involved an investor couple I work with, Mike and Meg. I assisted in helping them find and purchase 12 rental properties in Barrie, Ontario. All 12 properties were purchased and offered as rent-to-owns. They bought these properties one at a time. With one of their 12 properties, about two years into the tenancy, the tenants who were in the property decided that they wanted to move to Toronto, closer to where the husband worked. The tenants forfeited the rent-to-own agreement and moved to Toronto. Two years later, these very same tenants reached back out to Mike and Meg and said they realized Toronto wasn't for them and they wanted to move back to Barrie. The house they were originally in when they lived in Barrie was already occupied by another tenant. Mike and Meg went out and purchased another property for these tenants so that they could do the rent-to-own program again on this new property. Keep in mind, this means that these tenants originally forfeited their down payment plus all the credit, moved out of the house, then reached out to those investors years later asking to get back into the rent-to-own program again for a second time, providing another option payment for the investors.

Who are these tenants who choose rent-to-own?

Tenants who choose to do rent-to-own are often people that have one or more of the following roadblocks that prevent them from qualifying for a mortgage with a bank or credit union: poor credit, a divorce that caused bad debt from the ex, they are new to the country and haven't established credit, business owners who are not properly reporting income with Canada Revenue, an individual who may have claimed bankruptcy years ago and since improved their situation drastically, or seasonal workers and other hardworking people who simply do not have enough money to qualify to purchase a home although they have decent income. As investors, we look for tenants who are stable in their jobs, who have the financial ability to pay rent and the desire to own a home. Although they can't qualify presently, they can in fact qualify for the home two to three years down the road if they do everything the mortgage broker tells them to do.

When a tenant successfully completes the rent-to-own program, the sale is considered to be a private sale between the investor and the tenant. There are no commissions to be paid to a realtor by the investor; we help with this. If the tenant does not complete the rent-to-own program and walks away from the home, the tenant forfeits all the monthly credit and the option payment. This leaves the investor free to do whatever he or she wants with the property, for example, offering the property as a rent-to-own rental again and collecting another option payment, offering the property as a regular rental, or selling the property. The investor can do whatever they like with the property because they still own it.

Conclusion

The great thing about being an investor offering a rent-to-own is that you're making money, but you're also doing something that improves the life of an entire family. You're helping them achieve their dream of homeownership when there is no other way they could have accomplished this dream. For the investor, a big incentive to start with a rent-to-own is that this strategy can be a huge catalyst to accumulate funds that the investor can use towards a down payment for their next property purchase.

Single-family properties

Boring will make you rich!

A single-family home can include several types of properties. The features of the home that we look for in an investment property are relatively similar regardless of the type of home: three to four bedrooms with one to two full bathrooms. The more bedrooms and full baths, the better usually, because it caters to a much larger tenant demographic, such as a family with a couple of children or teens, multi-generation families where a couple may have one or both of their parents living with them, and tenants who work from home and require an office.

I started off my portfolio purchasing single-family homes. I first purchased in Oakville and then gradually extended my purchases to just outside of Oakville. Today, I invest in property in seven different cities across Southern Ontario so far.

I chose to start with single-family homes around the golden horseshoe because in good economic times or bad, starter homes are always in demand. Shelter (housing) is not a want but is rather one of our most basic fundamental human needs, just like food. Starter properties have the most interest from both renters and buyers due to their affordability. Families can purchase these homes for themselves to live in, and investors can easily purchase and rent them out. Unlike higher end homes, starter homes will always be in demand regardless of market conditions. In bad economic times, higher end luxury real estate is typically the first type of home in the housing market to take a hit due to a lack of buyers.

Starter homes around Southern Ontario are also much easier to find compared to multi-residential investment properties simply because there are much more of these types of homes available for sale in the market. This means you can scale this category quite quickly as an investor.

Tidal wave

In Canada we have a tidal wave of millennials coming down the pipeline that need housing, over 7.3 million for a fact. Millennials will quickly outnumber baby boomers (our aging population). Many millennials (people born between 1981 and 1996) are now starting families. They are starting to move out of their parents' basements or the small condo or apartment they are renting to more spacious, starter homes, usually a townhome, stacked townhome, semi or detached home for added space for their growing family. I strongly feel a good portion of millennials are going to be renting for life and not care to be homeowners. They will quickly become the largest generation of renters in our lifetime. Many of them have already chosen not to buy homes for various reasons: they can't come up with the down payment, homes are just too expensive for where they want to live, lifestyle preferences such as the desire to not sacrifice as much as generations before them have but to instead enjoy leisure trips, eating out, entertainment, etc. Many millennials will choose to live a renter lifestyle that gives them more flexibility. Many, by choice, won't own a home or a car but have access to everything through renting: Uber, Lyft, SkipTheDishes, Uber Eats. I am not trying to stereotype here or say what is right or what is wrong, I'm just sharing my knowledge from the market and the conversations that I have when speaking with millennials.

Better tenants

You may have heard that most landlords prefer tenants for single-family homes as they believe these tenants are better quality than the tenants you get in duplexes or apartments. From the thousands of properties I have helped investors purchase, from single-family homes all the way to large apartment buildings, I don't think it is a fair statement to suggest one type of tenant is better than the other. It's just like rent-to-own tenants; they may or may not be better than regular rental tenants. I have great tenants in multi-residential properties and great tenants in single-family properties. I've had a couple of undesirables in single-family properties and the same in multi-residential properties.

However, there is a difference when it comes to collecting rent payments. Usually, in the case of a single-family home, at least two people in the household are working, i.e. the mom and dad. If one of them temporarily loses their job, there is still income coming in from the other to support the family and pay rent. If you have a single person living in an apartment unit and he or she loses their job, there is now zero income coming in from this individual. So, with a single-family home, you are more likely to get your rent payment when it is due if something like a job loss occurs.

Tenant turnover is also slower when it comes to single-family homes. This boosts rental profits because these properties experience fewer vacancies, meaning you'll have less downtime with no money coming in.

Furthermore, once a family gets established in a single-family home, they tend to rent for a minimum of five years on average. This is often because, just like regular homeowners, you just don't want to uproot your family and be moving from neighbourhood to neighbourhood every couple of years. Routines would need to change because of the move. The family would need to find new restaurants, gyms, parks, schools, and stores, and their children would need to make new friends.

I'm currently on a 10-year run of not having a single day's vacancy with any of our single-family homes. What has always happened is that the tenants occupying the house would be courteous enough to give us the required 60 days' notice when moving out. Often, the tenants would even give us more than 60 days' notice. Once the tenant has given us notice that they will be moving out of the property, my wife immediately puts the home up for rent on Kijiji and other social sites we use to advertise our properties. New prospective tenants respond to the ads and we set up appointments to show the home while the current tenant is still living in the house. If a new tenant likes the home, they fill out an application. We do background checks and have our selected tenants sign a lease contract and provide us with a minimum of the last month's rent, but ideally the first month's rent as well. The tenants are not required to pay the first month's rent 'till the day they move in, but we always feel a little more comfortable if we have the first and last month's rent in hand and not have to think about collecting rent on the day they move in. This means we have one tenant moving out and the new tenant moving in the very next day. If required, we can make updates and small repairs to the house while either the old tenant is in the house or when the new tenant has just moved in. We have always been able to make it work with the tenants so that it is a smooth transition for everyone.

One of the advantages of single-family homes is that you are dealing with one family. When dealing with one family, you are hardly ever getting any calls from your tenants. When dealing with multi-residential properties though, you almost feel like you need a psychology degree sometimes. You will get incessant calls: upset tenants complaining about a baby crying in another unit, excessive dog barking, the smell of smoke, loud music, someone is not picking up after their dog in the backyard, another tenant didn't park properly in the driveway, and the list goes on.

Appreciation

Another advantage of single-family homes is that historically, single-family properties have appreciated much faster than multi-family homes. Usually, the value of single-family homes is determined by supply and demand. In Southern Ontario, there is much more demand than supply for these types of properties. Multifamily property values are based on their condition and the rents being collected. This means the value of multi-family homes typically rises when rents go up for that building or in the area, and they don't follow the trends of appreciation that single-family homes do in the same area.

Fewer expenses, repairs, and maintenance

Single-family homes are also often associated with fewer expenses than multi-family homes. For example, investors of multi-family homes are usually responsible for paying utility bills which, ultimately, will add on to their rental expenses and cut into their cash flow, especially if tenants' utility consumption is excessive. It's extremely rare for all utilities to be paid by the tenants in multi-residential homes. If this can be done that is great. But usually, they are only responsible to pay rent and hydro. With single-family homes, the tenants are 100% responsible for covering the full cost of utilities.

We also have to consider the maintenance and repairs of a multi-family home. If multiple repairs are required (for example multiple balconies, a flat roof, underground parking, the boiler system, etc.), these are huge expenses that the investor has to pay for. With single-family homes, the cost of repairs is usually much smaller. Fixing 10 windows instead of 1000 windows is much less expensive.

With multi-family properties, an investor would most likely want and pay for a property management company to manage the building. But single-family homes usually do not require property management. This eliminates the property management cost and increases cash flow.

Conclusion

Considering the stable rental income, longer tenancy, less costly repairs, strong appreciation over time, less management, fewer calls and monthly expenses—single-family homes typically have a better chance of generating positive cash flow and requiring less money to manage and maintain.

Investors I work with and I will pass on way more deals than we invest in. Many offers we make are turned down by the seller. It is common for sellers to believe their property is worth more than the market will bear. Sellers of single-family homes often have a personal connection with the home and have a tough time separating emotion from business when they put their home up for sale. As a result, asking prices can be high, and offers below the asking price are often turned down. That is just a reality of real estate investing. We probably purchase less than 3% of the properties we look at. On paper and online, the property may look great. But physically getting to the property and seeing it up close will reveal the full story: compromised foundations or structural issues, asbestos or UFFI in the home, dated or comprised electrical wiring, galvanized plumbing instead of copper, too many of the majors such as the roof, furnace, AC, or windows in need of repair, the junkyard neighbour who has a half-dismantled car in their driveway, or a vicious, annoying barking dog that is outside all day. When purchasing a single-family home, besides looking at the fundamentals of the area, one should also consider what the demand will be for the property in five, 10, 20 years from now. What areas are going to be the most in demand? I can't stress how vitally important it is to know your market and choose the right property. Choosing the wrong property in the wrong area can quickly sour a first-time investor who may never get into the market again.

Second suite properties

Second suite properties, sometimes referred to as accessory apartments, two-unit dwellings, or duplexes, are very popular amongst investors looking for the best use of a single-family home and high cash flow. With Southern Ontario housing prices continuing to appreciate and single-family dwellings being the hottest commodity of all real estate, it's no wonder why investors are aggressively searching for homes where the basement, attic, garage, or lot can accommodate additional living space.

Recently, the Ontario government, realizing Ontarians' desperate need for affordable housing, implemented Bill 140, the 'Strong Communities through Affordable Housing Act'. The implementation of this Act gave the majority of cities and towns across Ontario the authority to encourage and allow second suite units to be constructed. This provision assists with the government's goal of providing affordable housing in Ontario.

Benefits of second suite properties to investors and tenants

A legal second suite property is defined as a separate residence inside, attached to, or within the lot of what once was a single-family residential home. This second unit has its own sleeping, bathroom, and kitchen facilities. The majority of secondary suites are basement suites, but they can also be additions to the original property, converted garage spaces, or redesigned side splits. For the owner of this type of property, cash flow is significantly increased. Tenants benefit because they get a large living space with a backyard for a similar rent that they would pay for an apartment or condo. The tenants would also be being paying less rent than they would if they were renting a single-family home. These homes are also most often found in more established neighbourhoods; near schools, shopping centers, recreational facilities, parks, restaurants, and other important amenities. These types of units often have a garage for additional storage space, which is another luxury for the tenants and not usually an option when renting a condo or apartment.

Desirable second suite properties

A turnkey converted second suite property usually costs roughly $150,000 more than a single-family home. The buyer is basically paying for the convenience of not having to go through the process and costs of the conversion from single-family home to second suite property themselves.

Investors who purchase a single-family home and go through the process of converting it to a legal second suite will produce typical cash flow of anywhere between $1,000 to $1,450 per month after all expenses. Using one of our properties as an example, my wife and I purchased a 1960s 1350 sq. ft. three-bedroom, two-bath bungalow in the north end of one of the most desirable areas of Brantford, Ontario. Our purchase price was $342,500. The majors such as the roof, furnace, AC, windows, electrical, and plumbing came updated when we purchased the home; all done by the previous owner. The main floor was updated, except for the bathroom. The basement was extremely dated, which was no problem for us because we had the full intention to gut it and convert it to a legal second suite.

We spent a total of $109,000 on the conversion and updates. That covered the cost of gutting the original basement, converting it into a brand-new two bed, full bath, open concept living room and kitchen with all appliances and a separate laundry. This also included updating the main floor bathroom, widening the driveway, installing new exterior handrails and cutting the concrete foundation to enlarge the basement windows to meet natural light requirements for the lower unit. The renovation took us roughly three months to complete. Because the main floor was pretty much turnkey when we purchased the property, we started with the main floor bathroom renovation right away, and it took only two days to complete. We also advertised and filled the main floor unit days after closing on the property. We had the main floor tenant agree and sign a contract that laid out the details of the construction that was going to take place in the lower unit: 9 am to 6 pm, Monday to Saturday, and it would take roughly three months to complete.

Right away we had the main floor tenant's entry to the basement drywalled so that there would be no intrusion or dust into their main floor unit while the construction to the lower unit was taking place.

In return for the main floor tenants having to live through the inconvenience of construction in the lower unit, we reduced their rent by a couple of hundred bucks until the job was completed. The tenants were usually not home, as they worked during the majority of the hours that construction was taking place at the property. It was pretty much a win-win for them and for us; they paid a little less rent for the minor inconvenience, and we were able to get a family in paying rent, which helped to lower our carrying costs until construction was finished and our lower tenant moved in.

Three months later, our second suite was completed. If we did not do the renovation and convert the basement to a second suite, our property would have rented out as a single-family home to one family for $1,900 plus utilities. Having converted it into two units, we receive $3,325 in monthly rental income for this property ($1,800 rent for the main floor and $1,425 for the lower unit) all inclusive. Utilities never end up being over $300 per month, and when we factor in the cost of property tax and insurance, we end up with cash flow of a little over $1,400 per month for this one property.

We created instant equity, making the market value of the property worth more than our original purchase price. We could have refinanced the property, pulled all our renovation money out, and reinvested that money into the next property and go through the exact same process again. This is often referred to as the brrrr strategy: buy, renovate, rent, refinance, and repeat. We get into this in Chapter 4.

Our original down payment for the property was $68,500 (20% of the purchase price of $342,500). We paid $109,000 for the conversion and updates. After the renovation was completed, the market value was not $451,500 (our purchase price $342,500 plus our renovation costs $109,000). In fact, that property was now worth closer to $575,000. We literally forced the value of the property up $232,500 by doing a $109,000 renovation. At this point, what some investors do is refinance the property. In that case, an appraiser goes into the property to verify the work done. The appraiser then provides the bank with a new market value of the property. In our case, the market value would have been $575,000. The bank will then allow the investor to take up to 80% of the value of the home minus the current mortgage. Our market value of $575,000 x 80% minus our outstanding mortgage balance of $274,000 = $186,000. We could have refinanced this home, taken out our initial down payment of $68,500 as well as the $109,000 we used to renovate, and owned the property for zero dollars out of pocket while still being ahead an additional $8,500 and using the $186,000 towards our next property. You can quickly see how this brrrr strategy is becoming popular with investors.

Another alternative would have been to flip the property. We could have completed the property and put it on the market for another family or investor to buy, making a profit of a little over $120,000 in three months. However, the idea of flipping is not part of our long-term goals. We rather buy and hold for the long-term.

What makes a great second suite property?

Second suite conversions can be done with semis, townhomes, and detached properties. From our experience and working with hundreds of investors and tenants, bungalows built anywhere between 1960 and 1980 often end up being the best candidates for conversions to second suite properties. Usually, these homes have a 1,000 sq. ft. main floor area or greater. They already have a second entrance that is usually off the side or back of the house with immediate access to stairs leading to the basement (our separate entrance). The basement is usually the same size as the main floor; 1000 sq. ft. or greater. The lots are usually quite big, often 50' x 100'. The properties are often set back from the city sidewalk or road enough so that we can accommodate legal parking requirements. This gives us the opportunity to have two units of 1000 sq. ft. or larger, an already existing second entrance, a large backyard to share, and appropriate parking for our tenants and their vehicles.

Zoning

The last thing you want when purchasing a property that you plan on converting to a second suite is to find out that you cannot convert it, either due to the zoning restrictions of the neighbourhood or something to do with the home itself.

Just because a single-family home may meet the proper zoning requirement, that doesn't necessary mean that the home can be converted to legal second suite property. The property itself might conflict with the bylaws or the Ontario building code requirements. Investors who plan to renovate and convert a property to a second suite should first call the city to find out if zoning permits this type of property conversion. But even if the city says that the property address does fall within the zoning that allows a two-unit dwelling, that is not enough information. It would be a very bad idea to purchase a property just because it looks good and has the permitted zoning requirement. You don't want to purchase a property and then get stopped at the planning department because the property itself does not support a second suite conversion. This could happen for many reasons, for example the lot cannot accommodate the necessary parking requirements, the basement ceiling height is too low, or the square footage of the unit is too big or too small. A buyer not knowing any better may have their plans of a second suite property come to a grinding halt. The buyer would then be stuck with a property they probably would not have purchased if they had known these things before purchasing.

Secondary suites make for excellent investment properties, but the investor needs to know or be working with someone who knows building codes, bylaws, and zoning before they go out and purchase a property they plan on converting. These conversions need to be built on lots that have the zoning allowance, meet Ontario building code requirements, and also comply with the city or town bylaws. The Ontario building code is the same across Ontario. However, the bylaws for these builds are different from city to city and town to town. For instance, at this present time the maximum square footage of a secondary unit in St. Catharines Ontario is 650 sq. ft. This means that you are often left with 350 to 400 sq. ft. in the basement that you have to figure out what to do with. In Hamilton, the unit can be no smaller than 700 sq. ft. What is allowed in one town might be illegal in the next town over.

Finding and purchasing a second suite property

Once we find a property for sale that we feel would make a good second suite property, we make an offer on the property. We know the different cities' bylaws, zoning, and Ontario building code requirements. However, as added protection, we put a condition in our offer that the offer is conditional upon a home inspection. We have three full-time home inspectors that we work with who have something that 99.9% of home inspectors do not have: their BCIN (Building Code Identification Number). This is the province of Ontario's way to recognize that a person is qualified and they understand the Ontario building code enough to be able to produce permit drawings and documents to submit to the city. One of the guys we work with was a city building inspector for over 30 years. A couple of the other inspectors we work with have the current city inspectors' cell numbers and sometimes call them from the property we are thinking about purchasing to get answers to questions we might have before we go firm on the property.

During our inspection with our inspector who has their BCIN, we can confidentially catch anything that we may have missed during our original walkthrough of the property that could put us at risk or give us problems in converting the property to a legal second suite property. If we discover an issue that we can't resolve to comply with requirements or that would simply be too expensive to resolve, we can cancel the deal based on the results of the home inspection. We walk away from the deal, and no money is lost. However, if the house passes the inspection, we now have the inspector with their BCIN license that can do the permit drawings for the buyer.

The conversion drawings are designed and brought to the city to show that the unit we want to build complies with the Ontario building code and the city's bylaws. The designer makes sure that we meet all the requirements for parking, unit and lot size, ceiling height, proper egress, smoke detectors and alarms, fire doors, fire separation, natural light, etc. The plan's adherence to these requirements will be reviewed by the city's planning examiner.

The process of a second suite conversion

It typically takes two to three weeks for the city to review the permit drawings and give approval for the renovations to start. It may take a little longer if there are any issues that will require revisions to the drawings. Once the city gives you approval, they will give you a permit document that you have to post on a front window at the property to show that you're actually doing work under permit. Without this permit, a neighbour can quickly call the city and have the site shut down. The permit shows you have the city's approval and you're allowed to do the work that you're proposing to do. During construction, there will be various stages where the city inspector will need to come in and review the work before you can go on to the next stage. For instance, the city inspector will need to come by to review framing and plumbing. The Electrical Safety Authority will also need to inspect the electrical. This all has to be done before drywall goes up. This is why it is so important to use a contracting team that has done this type of construction before. Otherwise, if the unit is drywalled before those inspections are passed, the city will request that all drywall is torn out for inspections to be done. The drywall would then need to be reinstalled again and the mistake would prove costly.

We work with multiple contracting teams that specialize in second suite unit conversions. It's super handy having these guys in our network because with their experience and expertise, we don't fall behind schedule because something was missed during the renovation.

Before you can officially fulfill all the open permit obligations, a final occupancy inspection will take place where the city inspector will confirm all work is completed and everything complies as per the drawings. Then you would get your occupancy permit and can officially rent out the property.

Renovations

If you are either gutting the basement or working from a clean slate, this is not the time to cut corners. Anyone can draw out two bedrooms, a bath, kitchen, and separate laundry in a rectangular box. With the right design, you will not only command top dollar in rent, you will command top dollar in resale value down the road. You usually want a beautiful, bright open-concept kitchen with stainless steel appliances. The kitchen should ideally open up to the living area. The flooring throughout this space should be consistent and one colour, usually a decent quality vinyl plank flooring that looks like hardwood. Vinyl plank flooring has come such a long way over the years and is much more durable than any other type of material. Using the same type of flooring through the kitchen and living area gives the space the illusion of looking larger. Using two different materials chops up the area and makes the unit look smaller. Investing in decent washroom fixtures and appliances will also help save you money over time. The goal is to use materials to make the property look inviting, bright, and tenant proof so that when you refill or sell the property one day, it doesn't look tired or dated. Instead, with a quick clean and freshen-up, it will look as good as new.

Tips

We have helped investors complete hundreds of second suite conversions across Southern Ontario. As I write this book, we have a couple of properties in various stages of being turned into second suite properties. Some of the properties being converted right now are in London, Barrie, St. Catharines, Brantford, Hamilton, and Guelph.

When it is time to convert a property to a legal second suite, we submit the drawings to the city to apply for a permit before even owning the home. When we get an offer accepted on the property, a seller typically needs 30 to 90 days before they are going to move out of the home they sold. After our offer is accepted, we get the drawings done in a couple of days and submit them to the city. This helps to drastically cut down the total time it takes from taking possession of the property to completing the secondary unit and getting the occupancy permit. This way, the city approves the drawings in time for us to start construction on day one of ownership as opposed to closing on the property, getting the drawings done, waiting for the city's approval, hoping there is no back and forth with the drawings, which can easily burn up an additional four to six weeks of carrying a vacant home without being able to do any work to it.

When the drawings are being done for the second suite, you want to make sure that the unit is as functional and attractive as possible. The ideal second suite property has three bedrooms up and two bedrooms down each unit with their own full bath, kitchen, and laundry. This is where you really extract value and get higher rent. Fewer rooms and space in a home will typically command lower rent because they are smaller units. A double wide driveway with tandem parking (so four cars total) would also make for an ideal property because there is ample parking. If the property does not have a garage, you definitely want to install two sheds side by side in the backyard, one for each unit. These sheds come in really handy for tenants. They can put their seasonal furniture in there, as well as bikes, winter tires, and anything else they need to store.

Alternatively, you could also purchase a property that has second suite potential and not do the second suite conversion immediately after closing. You could purchase a single-family bungalow now and only consider the conversion further down the road after enough equity has been built up in the home. Giving yourself options to generate higher cash flow at a future date is advanced real estate investment thinking.

What to do if the property doesn't meet the bylaw requirements 100%

Not all properties are going to be the perfect property where you can simply go to the city with drawings and get a permit to commence the build of a legal second suite. If something does not meet a bylaw requirement, for instance, you don't have the required width driveway, a minor variance would need to be applied for.

The minor variance process is when you formally ask the city for permission to do something outside of what is written in the bylaw. In regard to second suite parking, for instance, the bylaw requires one parking space per unit and a certain size per parking stall.

Sometimes the lot size of the property doesn't allow this much space, so you need to apply for a variance for a reduction. Other times you may need to widen the parking area, but the city wants 50% of the front yard landscaped, i.e. grass opposed to hardscape driveway. To apply for a variance, you or your designer would fill out city forms, swear oath, pay the application fee of $1,500 to $2,500, and submit your documents. Neighbours will receive a letter in the mail from the city with details of your minor variance application and what exactly you are applying for. The city will then provide you with a sign to be placed at the front of the property where the public can see it and make note of the contact information should they wish to make inquiries. That sign must remain posted beginning 21 days prior to the hearing, until the day following the hearing.

A few weeks later, the application is heard in front of the committee of adjustment. At the hearing, neighbours have an opportunity to comment on your application. I've been to many of these hearings and have never seen a neighbour come in to comment on an application for a variance related to a second suite property. For the neighbours to get up in arms and attend one of these hearings, something much more significant would usually be going on, for example if the neighbourhood golf course is bought by a developer who wants to build three condo towers amongst surrounding two-story homes. Homeowners don't want these massive buildings in their backyard, therefore they would attend the hearing to voice their concerns. There the city officials would decide whether or not the complaint is valid and if construction can or cannot take place.

Conclusion

Second suite properties are incredibly popular on the resale market and buyers tend to pay a premium price for these types of properties. Investors are attracted to this type of property because it generates instant cash flow. Regular and first-time home buyers are interested as well because they can purchase a home that would work well with in-laws, or they could also rent a portion of the house out themselves as a mortgage helper to help lower their personal monthly payments by almost a half.

Converting a single-family home to a legal second suite property definitely requires specific knowledge and quite a bit of work, but they tend to be incredibly profitable for investors and therefore a very popular investment strategy.

Multi-family properties

What you don't know will hurt you!

Single-family properties are residential buildings with only one available unit to rent, while multi-family properties have more than one unit under one roof. Second suite properties are technically 'multi-family properties', but in all fairness, I felt I couldn't do the topic of second suites justice if I lumped them in with our multi-family section.

Given the popularity of second suites, I felt they needed special attention.

Here, we will discuss additional types of multi-family properties and the motivations as to why these types of properties are great additions to an investor's real estate portfolio.

Multi-family properties contain two or more units, such as a duplex or triplex all the way up to apartment buildings that can contain hundreds of units. The primary advantage of multi-family properties is diversified income for the investor. In the case of a single-family home, if your tenant vacates your property, you are responsible for 100% of the costs while the property is vacant: mortgage, property tax, insurance. But if one tenant were to vacate a 10-unit multi-family property, you would only be 10% out of rent (one unit vacant, nine other units tenanted), a fractional portion of rent not coming in compared to a vacant single-family home. This scenario is one of the main motivations why investors choose multi-family properties.

Determining the value of a multi-family property

The decision to purchase a single-family home or a student rental is quite easy. The buyer can determine whether the seller's asking price is fair by simply looking at comparable sales of similar properties in the area. Determining the value of a multi-family property requires a little more work. There are a couple of approaches we can use to determine the market value of these properties. One method is much like our method to determine the value of a single-family home, and that is a comparative market analysis. A comparative market analysis looks at similar buildings ('comps') that have recently sold to arrive at a value. It's important to note that this method does not consider the income and expenses of the building, which is important. It only looks at what similar multi-family properties in the area have sold for.

The more commonly used method to determine the value of multi-family properties is determining the cap rate of the property and comparing that number to other cap rates of multi-family properties in the area. This method is most often used by Realtors, appraisers, bankers, and insurers such as CMHC (Canada Mortgage and Housing Corporation) to determine the value of multi-family properties. The cap rate is determined by dividing the net operating income (NOI) by the property value to arrive at a percentage. For example, if a property was listed for $1,000,000 and generated a NOI of $60,000, the cap rate would be 6%. Net operating income is calculated by using the total income generated from the property and subtracting the expenses. For instance, adding up all rental income and any other revenue such as coin laundry, paid parking, and storage, and then subtracting operating costs associated with running and maintaining the property, such as utilities, property management, taxes, repairs, and maintenance. The expenses used exclude the mortgage principle and interest payments.

With multi-family properties, the cap rate would be used to measure profitability and to compare to other properties currently listed for sale or that have sold in the area to determine the value of the property. If we are analyzing a property with a cap rate of 5.5% and most properties sell at approximately a 5% cap rate, it's very possible that the property in question is well priced and a good deal. Conversely, if we are analyzing a property and the result is a 3% cap rate while most properties sell at a 5% cap rate in the area, it's very possible the property in question is overpriced and not a good deal.

When analyzing the economics of a marketplace in general, a down trend in cap rates over time generally means that property prices are increasing, demand is strong, and the market is doing well. Going back in time and analyzing historical cap rate data is a great way to understand where the market has been and where it could be going.

What makes a good multi-family property?

While each deal may be different, the overall elements in the examining and purchasing of a multi-family property are pretty much the same, just on a different scale. Before we decide if a multi-family property is worth physically going to view, we always request and examine the property's financial data (income and expenses), more commonly referred to as the property pro forma in the investment world. By analyzing these numbers, we can determine if the property is near or below market value and whether or not the property should be investigated further.

An investor can increase the value of a multi-family property by either increasing the income and/or reducing the operating expenses. This increases the net operating income, thereby increasing the value of the property. The most desirable multi-family properties are often ones where the units can be upgraded as tenants vacate, so that the rental income for the unit can be increased. In a single-family home, we can do a renovation to the property to command higher rent and make the property more valuable, however, we are doing this to force the appreciation and rental income of one property only. If we update a multi-family property and make it more appealing; i.e. renovate and update units, add or upgrade a laundry room, revitalize unused space to create something beneficial, or add an extra unit, we will increase the value of the property as we can now command higher rental income. These upgrades and benefits also help with steadier cash flow because the tenants will want to stay in our properties longer.

Lowering the operating expenses of a property also renders it more valuable and profitable. Some common, inexpensive ways to reduce operating expenses include reducing water bills with low flow fixtures for shower heads and toilets or reducing electrical usage by either sub-metering units or replacing light fixtures with LED bulbs.

Location

Location always has a significant impact on the choices we make when purchasing an investment property. Keeping an eye out and being able to identify a great deal in a desirable location is half the battle. It's important to choose your location wisely when buying a multi-family property. The location should be a good, safe community, near schools, hospitals, convenience stores, fast food, grocery stores, and especially public transit. Talk with the existing tenants when you view the property. This way you'll get to know who you'll be dealing with if you were to become the owner of the property. Tenants are a great source of information. If you ask respectfully, I find tenants will tell you what they like or dislike about an area and what they like or dislike about the property. Tenants can be our best allies when purchasing a property. If they are huge fans of the property, that is obviously a good sign. If they rattle off a laundry list of issues with the property or area, that may mean we should move on to the next property and keep looking.

Property management

I find most investors like to have any multi-family properties from five units and up property managed rather than managing them themselves. With a single-family home, you only have to deal with one family. In a multi-family property of five or more units, you have multiple personalities to deal with, and they may not always get along with each other. You will have to intervene in squabbles and complaints. An investor who has the money to qualify for five units or greater usually does not have time for these calls. In this case, property management would be the way to go. A good property management company can take calls from tenants, show, lease, and collect rent while maintaining the overall property.

Qualifying to purchase

When a buyer purchases a multi-family property, the banks often allow the buyer to use rental income from the other units to offset their personal income and boost the purchase price of the property that the investor can qualify to purchase. A buyer that may qualify to purchase a $500,000 single family home may be able to qualify to purchase a $750,000 multi-family property because the rents are being used by the lender to increase the buyer's purchasing power. Multi-family homes with up to four units are considered residential for the purpose of financing. You can buy them with mortgages just like those used to buy single-family homes. But multi-family properties with five or more units are considered multi-family commercial mortgages and require commercial real estate loans. Mortgages for commercial real estate are generally more difficult to get and require bigger down payments of between 25% to 30%, compared to single-family investments that only require a 20% down payment.

Another consideration when purchasing a multi-family property is that when it comes to acquisition costs, investors should budget for costs related to environmental assessments (a possible Phase I or Phase II inspection), as well as in-depth inspections of the mechanical, heating, and air conditioning systems. These items can be costly to repair and should not be overlooked when purchasing one of these properties.

Conclusion

Single-family and multi-family properties both offer strong benefits to the investor over time. The decision to purchase single-family or multi-family ultimately depends on your short-term objectives, long-term goals, and what you can qualify to purchase, knowing that one requires more work than the other. In the multi-family space, there is definitely less competition from homeowners as they are not usually looking to purchase these; only investors are.

Student Rentals

Where's the party?

A student rental income property can be a semi, townhome, detached home, condo, or building. The main motivation for an investor to purchase a student rental is high cash flow. These homes, which are rented by the room, can have from one or two bedrooms all the way up to 12 bedrooms or more in a single home, depending on the city and the bylaws. When newbie investors hear student rentals, they often think party house, backyard parties full of garbage, and damage to the home. In my over 20 years of real estate investing experience, I have gone through thousands of student rentals and maybe seen a handful of homes that were neglected. But you could easily tell by the state of these homes that they were most likely owned by an absentee landlord who never did any updates to the home and never took proper care of maintenance or repairs. When you have a few nicks in the floors or scratches and dings on the wall…what's an extra scratch or another nick? With a good student rental that is properly managed and taken care of, a scratch in the floor or nick in the wall would stick out like a sore thumb.

One of the many strategies we use to help keep our student rental properties in great shape and avoid damages is to get parental guarantees signed by the students' parents. Each and every parent signs a parental guarantee stating that the parents are responsible for all damages and losses to the landlord. The parents are then liable for any damages as well any rental arrears, charged to the parents as their prorated share. For example, if there are five named tenants on the lease agreement, the guarantors (each set of parents), in addition to each of the students, would be liable for 20% of any damages and rental arrears. Each family being responsible for 20% means the owner can recoup the full 100%.

You know what is great about student rentals? Rent! For a single-family home, we typically have two people responsible for rent. The two people typically responsible is the couple who signed the lease. Both are probably gainfully employed, and they are the only ones we can expect to pay rent. For a five-bedroom student rental, for example, we have 15 people responsible for rent—five students plus their parents. You will get paid!

Location, location, location

If you live in Ontario, you are in close proximity to the majority of the top universities and colleges in Canada. Student rentals provide an excellent return on investment and are a great way to diversify one's real estate portfolio. A single-family home that may rent to a family for $1,900 to $2,000 can often rent for double that price as a student rental. To command top rent for our properties, as with any real estate investment, location is key.

As investors, the criteria that we look for in a single-family home is not the same criteria that makes a great student rental investment. Each university has different 'key locations' or 'zones', and the criteria that makes a location or property great for one university may not be the same for another university. For example, one of the most desired neighbourhoods for McMaster University in Hamilton is an area known as 'Westdale'. The distance from Westdale to the university campus is approximately 1 km, a 10 min walk, which is one of the reasons this area is so popular amongst students. But the number-one reason students want to live in this particular area is because the majority of desired amenities for students are located here; restaurants, fast-food, pubs, gyms, Shoppers Drug Mart, groceries, convenience stores, and coffee shops. As a result, students will pay a premium to live in this location. South of Main St. W, directly across the street from the campus and also within a 1 km radius, the housing properties are cheaper, and so are the rents students are willing to pay. These homes, even though they can be closer to the campus than the properties in Westdale, are considered less desirable and command lower rent because they are further away from the major amenities that the students desire to be close to. Both zones are great places to invest, you just need to know that properties that are the same distance to the university or even closer are not necessary more valuable. This will also be reflected in the amount of rent a student will be willing to pay and the amount of demand for these types of properties among students.

Conversely, if we look at the University of Western Ontario, many students prefer to be close to amenities that are located outside of the 1 km radius that McMaster students prefer. In this case, the radius of desirable locations is actually closer to 3 km from the university. One of the popular locations for students is the area of Richmond St. and Oxford St. E, closer to the downtown core of the city rather than the campus itself. Although this forces students to take public transit to get to and from campus, a good portion of students prefer this location as its within walking distance of the same types of amenities at the sacrifice of not being within walking distance of the campus. At Western, it's typically the graduate students, professors, and teacher's aides that like to live close to the campus and away from the bars and restaurants.

Brock University in St. Catharine's is another example. The most desirable area students tend to lean towards here is again not near the campus but rather close to the Pen Centre (Niagara's largest shopping center), in areas like the 'Village'. Living in this area, students are right near a ton of amenities inside the shopping center. It is also a place where many of them find part-time employment to help them pay for their university education. A student wouldn't make the walk from this location to the university because it would take them almost 45 minutes to get there. Instead, they use public transit that can get them from their rental to the campus in under 15 minutes.

The University of Guelph, University of Toronto, Queens, McGill, Waterloo, York, Ryerson, and others all have these preferred zones and less preferred zones that every investor should definitely know before purchasing a student rental property.

As Canadians, we also need to keep our climate in mind. For most students, except for those that take summer courses, courses run from the beginning of September 'till the end of April. Of those eight months, six or sometimes almost seven of those eight months are typically very frigid in the north. For a student to walk a couple of extra blocks to a bus stop or major amenities in our coldest temperatures of the year can make the difference between a good property or bad property. A student rental property located a couple of blocks in the wrong direction can make for a bad investment.

How many bedrooms are you legally allowed to have in your property?

Some cities have caps on how many bedrooms you can have in your student rental. There's nothing worse that hearing that someone purchased a student rental property because "the numbers looked good," until the city bylaw officer came by and stated that the owner had an illegal student rental: too many bedrooms under one roof. For instance, in the City of Guelph, you can only have a maximum of four bedrooms in a single-family home. In St. Catherine's, the cap is six, in London it's five, and Hamilton is presently a free-for-all. In Hamilton, five- and six-bedroom student rentals are the most common. In others there are more than 10 bedrooms! As an investor, you have to be working with (or know yourself) what the legal limit is for bedrooms under one roof per the city's bylaw before purchasing a student rental. Once the house gets red-flagged as having too many rooms, the bylaw officer will make sure you abide by the bylaw and you can be down one or two room rental incomes, which can quickly turn what looked like a good investment into not so great investment.

A student rental home that provides decent cash flow needs to be attractive to students. Students don't want to be jumping over one another to use a bathroom in the house. Therefore, a home with five to six beds should have at least two full bathrooms. If you have a six-bedroom student rental, the ideal layout would be a home with a separate entrance; one entrance opening up to a three-bedroom unit with a kitchen, living room (common area), and bathroom, and the second entrance possibly leading into the basement with the same setup. With seven or more bedrooms you 100% need a second kitchen and ideally a third full bathroom.

My wife and I own a three-bedroom one-bathroom home that was converted to a five-bedroom, five-and-a-half-bathroom student rental close to the University of Western. Each of the five bedrooms have their own individual ensuite bathroom. This is considered a luxury student rental and commands top rent.

More is not always better

The more bedrooms you have available, the greater the rental income the property can generate. However, we find that for our single-family home student rentals, once you try to fill eight rooms or more, it can be a little more challenging management and desirability wise. Although having so many rooms under one roof generates great cash flow, there is definitely more work required. Keep in mind that students come as a group when it is time to lease a property. For a student to gather a group of three to five friends to lease a property is not that difficult. But once it's eight or more, they are typically living with friends of a friend or someone they don't know well (or at all). Otherwise, the landlord or property management company needs to find a student here and there to fill vacant rooms. It can be done, but it is just not the ideal situation because you want to avoid students butting heads and having issues with one another. This is more likely to happen when they don't know one another versus if they come together as a group. When a group of students know one another, they are more likely to sort out problems amongst themselves. A group that doesn't really know one another is more likely to reach out to the owner or property management company for help and intervention when a neutral party is required—one of the students is being too loud, too messy, leaving their dishes in the sink, not taking their laundry out of the washer or dryer when their clothes are done, etc.

Health of the university

The health of a university should also be a major consideration before purchasing a student rental property. Is the number of students enrolling increasing or decreasing each year? Does the university have the funds and land to grow, to accommodate the build of new lecture facilities and research centers which would lead to an increase in student population therefore a greater demand for housing? Or is the university struggling financially; are they shutting down particular programs? This needs to be monitored yearly at a minimum, but ideally every month.

As an example, in 2015, after almost 50 years in Brantford Ontario, Mohawk College was shut down due to financial constraints. Those students, roughly 1,700, were relocated to the Mohawk College campus in Hamilton. That's potentially 1,700 fewer students needing housing in Brantford and 1,700 students now needing housing near the Hamilton campus. Although not all students live off campus in a student rental, the majority do not live at home with their parents and make the commute.

In real estate, one of the best places to be is where rental demand is high and supply low. Back in 2015, anyone with a student rental near Mohawk College in Hamilton gained another 1,700 potential renters in one semester. At the same time, if you had a student rental property in Brantford and it wasn't one of the better ones, you would have most likely had to rent the property to a family, getting almost half the rent you were getting for it as a student rental, or maybe even considered selling if the property was running too much of a deficit. This is why it's so important to know the health of the university before purchasing. Signs that a university might be struggling include declining enrollment, curriculum courses continually being cut, and decrepit buildings showing they can't keep up with maintenance and repairs. A university that is doing well will have a rising enrollment rate, new faculty and research buildings, and constant updates and maintenance of their current facilities.

How to buy a student rental

There are several different ways an investor can purchase a property and rent it out to students. An investor can purchase a property that already has students on a signed lease living in the property. An investor can also purchase a property that is or was a student rental, take vacant possession once the students finish their lease, and then find their own tenants. Another option is to purchase a single-family home and have it converted into a student rental property.

The price of housing, the current use, and the potential monthly cash flow will have an impact on an investor's decision on where to buy and what type of property to purchase. If the investor's son or daughter is going to a particular university, that might be the decision maker right there. The investor purchases a property for their son or daughter, who will reside in that house until they graduate. We help investors to do this for their families every year. Often, the investor gives their son or daughter the responsibility of managing the property while they are living in it. This is a great way for a young person to get into the business of investment real estate. Some parents have their child put up some of the money for the down payment of the purchase, and they then become a percentage share holder of that property. When the investor eventually sells the property, their son or daughter will get their fair share of the profit. Meanwhile, the son or daughter often lives in the property for free because the rental income from renting out the other bedrooms is usually more than enough to cover all expenses. After a four- or five-year education, this family will benefit by not having to pay another landlord rent for their son or daughter while they attend post-secondary. They also benefit from the mortgage being paid down for those years, property appreciation and any additional cash flow.

Whether the property is a turnkey student rental or a property you converted to a student rental, each of the bedrooms in these homes is usually rented individually. These homes most often consist of five or six bedrooms, with each bedroom renting for anywhere between $500 to $800 per room, resulting in very good cash flow.

At the present time, one of the least inexpensive student rental properties to purchase in a key 'zone' would be in St. Catharines for Brock University. Properties there are in the low $400,000 and rents are roughly $500 per room. With a six-bedroom house, that's $3,000 a month rental income on a $400,000 purchase price home, resulting in great positive cash flow for the investor.

If the same house is rented to a family, rent would typically be $1,900 to $2,000 per month plus utilities. But if it is a six-bedroom student rental renting for $600 per room, that comes to $3,600 per month instead of $1,900 to $2,000 per month. That's an extra $1600 a month you are getting in additional rent by just changing the use of the property and adding a couple of additional bedrooms.

For universities like Western, McMaster, Waterloo, and Guelph, the purchase price of these properties would be roughly $500,000 to $600,000, with rents ranging anywhere from $575 to $800 per room.

Another essential consideration when deciding whether or not a property is a good investment is how much cash flow there will be after all expenses. Student rentals require a little more management, therefore the return for that extra effort should be greater than an investment like a single-family home that requires less management. A good student rental purchase should cash flow anywhere between $600 on the low end to $1,700 on the high-end per month after all expenses are paid.

One strategy for greater cash flow and forced appreciation on a property is to purchase a single-family home and have that home converted to a student rental. We have done many of these types of conversions with investors for student rentals for universities like Western, Guelph, Brock, McMaster, and Laurier, as well as several colleges like Mohawk, Niagara, and Georgian College in Barrie. With the majority of these conversions, the investor would purchase a three-bedroom home with one or two bathrooms and a finished recreation room (rec room). Then, layout depending, they would convert the dining area to a fourth bedroom and add two additional bedrooms in the rec room. You've now converted a three-bedroom home into a six-bedroom student rental. Not only will the property bring in greater rental income, but the value of the property is also increased because of the greater income it is generating.

In Guelph, where the legal limit for bedrooms is four, we turned a three-bedroom two-bathroom home into a legal six-bedroom student rental. We found the perfect two-story home in a great location for students. The investor purchased the home for $365,000. The dining room was turned into a fourth bedroom, and the investor also attained the permit to build a legal, two-bedroom accessory apartment in the basement. This made for a total of six bedrooms. The property generated $3,160 in monthly rental income and cash flow was $1,555 per month after all expenses. The total cost of that renovation was roughly $80,000.

Depending on how busy an investor's schedule is, they may not want to go through the conversion of a property and deal with contractors and the city. In this case, another option is to buy a turnkey student rental. We have worked with builders across Southern Ontario for over 20 years. Some of the relationships we have formed have afforded us access to properties that are not listed on the Multiple Listing Service (MLS) and not available to any other Realtors in Canada. To this day, we work with builders that build purpose-built student rentals. A management company then fills the property with a group of students and manages the property for roughly $125 per month. These properties are then offered to us as off-market listings from the builder and we have first access to this inventory. These properties come brand new, fully leased, and fully property managed. It doesn't get any more turnkey than that. We are then able to offer these properties to investors we work with.

It's really that easy. Now that all the work has been done to these properties and there won't be any maintenance or repairs in the foreseeable future, these properties are a little more expensive and the cash flow a bit lower. Instead of being in the $1,400 to $1,500 range after all expenses, the cash flow will be closer to $800, which is still nothing to be disappointed with.

Leases

When purchasing a student rental, it is vital to know the lease cycle of the university. Most universities, but not all, have lease cycles running from May 1st to April 30th, while others may run September 1st to August 31st. These are 12-month leases. Although most students' courses run from the beginning of September to the end of April in any given year, these students are still paying rent in May, June, July, and August when they are probably not even in town and back home living with their parents. Since these are year-round leases for students, there is no gap in rental income over the summer for the owner.

If you have students who have graduated and are not renewing their lease, you need to know when the advertising and signing of leases start. For example, leases for properties around the University of Western in London and McMaster University in Hamilton run May 1st to April 30th. However, landlords advertise up to seven months earlier, i.e. November, December, and January. This is a critical time to remember. Keep in mind that most students are busy with midterms in March and April. After that, they go home for the summer. It's very important to have your lease signed before the rental window closes.

When getting a lease signed, parental guarantees are a must. Just knowing that their parents would get a call and be responsible for any damage or rent arrears makes the students proactive and cognizant to behave.

One of the things I always recommend to investors when we are putting an offer on a student rental is to select the property that has the largest bedrooms and smallest common area. Students practically live in their bedrooms. They need a bed to sleep in and a desk and chair to read and study at. Getting a property with large bedrooms is very attractive to students, since technically, their room is their living space, much like a bachelor apartment. Choosing a house with a small common area (living room) also deters them from group gatherings and parties. These students will go over to the house a few doors down that has the much bigger common area, party there, and then come back to your place to sleep.

A good thing to point out to the students and leave somewhere obvious like on top of the fridge is a binder with details for them such as the closest amenities, like pizza shops, grocery stores, banks, convenience stores, coffee shops, pharmacies, as well as the garbage and recycling pickup dates and times. If you're providing Internet service for them, you will want to give them that contact, a copy of their lease, and local bus routes and times.

If you choose to self-manage a student rental, it's a good idea to have a lock box on the property to secure keys in. This will save you from unnecessary travel time to handle small problems like a student locking him/herself out of their room or a contractor needing to get into the property. The investor can give out the lock box code so that the student or contractor can get access to the property without the investor having to make a special trip to the property. The next time the investor goes to the property, he/she can change the lock box code to ensure the students or contractors are not needlessly taking keys out of the lock box with the risk of misplacing them.

Trends and a competitive advantage

We are in communication with multiple property management companies weekly. We take that time to touch base and find out if there are any trends happening that we should be aware of as investors. Are rents increasing? Are most landlords doing rent plus utilities or all inclusive? Are landlords offering free Internet or is that on the students to pay for? How is leasing looking for that particular year? Are they noticing anything different, for example oversupply or undersupply of properties? Are students preferring a particular area?

One trend we noticed and quickly fixed was to do with five or more bedroom homes. In around 2014, we noticed that houses with five or more bedrooms and one fridge often led to some or all of the students having mini fridges in their bedrooms. They were doing this because they didn't have enough room for their items in that one kitchen fridge. To prevent five extra mini fridges in the house, especially if the owner is paying utilities, we started installing two fridges side by side in the kitchen, which immediately removed the need for these extra mini fridges.

To help get top rent and to show our places better, we started furnishing our common areas. We would add either sectionals or a sofa and love seat in the living room, as well as a coffee table and flat screen TV. We would purchase a table and chairs for the kitchen. Just those few items, pretty inexpensive nowadays, made our homes look better as soon as you walked in and it was one less thing the students had to worry about purchasing when they moved into our properties. Now they just had to purchase their own desk, chair, and bed, which we never purchase. No student or student's parents wants their son or daughter to use someone else's used mattress and bed.

Conclusion

Student rentals can make for fantastic investment properties, especially if the investor's main goal is high cash flow. They definitely require more management than a single-family home, but provide some of highest monthly cash flow returns when comparing to any other type of real estate investment.

Flipping

TV shows have really done a 'good job' glamourizing the outcome of people flipping properties. I know someone who is involved in the production of one of these shows very well as well as someone who was actually on a show that featured him and glamourized the profit made. I can confidentially tell you that both those people told me that the profit numbers shown on those shows are not accurate. They are much lower. After all, if people are not making money on these shows, they won't be on the air much longer. To me, the perceptions created by these shows is awful because it gives newbie individuals who want to get into real estate a false sense of hope. To be clear, there is money to be made in flipping, I am not saying there isn't. It's just not as easy as most TV shows make it out to be. Talk to someone who flips homes in real life; they will tell you.

If done properly, you can change the odds and increase your chances of making money through a flip. Flipping is not my favorite way of investing in real estate at all. I have helped many investors do flips who simply could not move their investment careers forward because of lack of money. They needed to accumulate enough profit from flipping to then use that profit to purchase, buy, and hold properties. But there is always a risk to flipping. Luckily, everyone that I have helped to flip properties has a made a profit. For some, the profits were tens of thousands of dollars, and for others it was over six figures of profit. Again, one reason I am not a huge fan of this strategy is because we cannot control market conditions. If the market turns, and it can turn quickly, a flipper can end up losing a lot of money. A house that was originally thought to sell for $600,000 can quickly go down to $550,000 if there is some kind of turmoil in the market. When you need to sell to move on and stop the bleeding of expenses, you may need to sell the property at a loss.

I am not claiming to be the greatest Realtor in the world always making my clients profits when flipping properties. But I haven't let anyone down yet when doing a flip, and that is partly because I have a strategy for flipping properties that almost guarantees, regardless of market conditions, that the person flipping the property can still sell at the original projected price, or at least very close to it. This strategy involves turning a regular single-family home into an investment property rather than lipsticking a home, putting it back on the market, and hoping a family falls in love with the new updates. Investment properties mostly get sold on their income. So, if the property is profitable, an investor will want that property. The more profitable the property is, the more investors will want it.

The ideal property we look to flip is somewhere between 30 to 60 years old and located in a good neighbourhood on a good street. These are often original owner homes. Sometimes they are estate sales where no updates were done to the home, but the house is in great shape with no structural issues. The perfect property to flip is often one with the 50-year-old kitchen, pink carpet, green or blue bathtubs, toilets and sinks with matching wall tiles. Get a house with wallpaper and you have found yourself a real gem! We look for a home that would turn off the regular would-be buyer but not someone looking to flip a property. The worst house on the best street is often ideal for the best flip. We then turn that single-family home into a second suite property or a student rental, depending on the location and the best use for that property. After the renovation is completed, we can offer the property for sale vacant or filled with tenants. Then we sell an income producing property as a student rental or two-unit home. The property is 100% turnkey for any investor or family that needs a mortgage helper to purchase. Even if there is a little turmoil in the real estate market and some property values come down, it will sell much easier than a single-family home will to a regular buyer.

Warning!

Warning! Flipping is literally a job. It's something most people getting into real estate want to get out of, not into. It can be a part-time or full-time job, but the majority of successful flippers are definitely putting full-time hours into their flips. The most successful people doing flips have multiple crews and multiple projects on the go with systems in place.

When it comes to flipping, I typically meet two types of people. The first type is the flippers who are burnt out, stressed out, tired of the flipping business, and feel they should have kept a few of their properties instead of selling them, which they needed to do in order to put that profit into the next property while supporting their family. The money they make from flipping a property is essentially another form of a pay cheque; it just takes a few months before they get paid. It's a great way to start and get a quick injection of cash, but it is not the best way to become wealthy. It's just another job and another pay cheque, and once that flip sells, the cash stops unless you get right back at it again.

The other type is the person who wants to get into flipping because they want to build up a nest egg in order to later get into buy and hold properties. Essentially, they need money. At first, they may lack sufficient savings or not have enough equity in their home to use towards multiple rental properties. Their short-term objective is to build up enough equity through flipping a few properties to then later purchase multiple buy and hold properties once enough profit has been attained from their flips.

I have been in high appreciation markets, down markets, and flat markets. No one has a crystal ball. Some of the highest appreciation numbers experienced in the property market in Southern Ontario was between 2014 and 2016. I saw flippers make a small fortune. The real estate market was on fire. Some areas saw appreciation in the double digits. I saw one sale in Oakville where the person purchased the property with the intent of tearing it down and building a custom home. Roughly 90 days later, once the buyer took possession, the property increased in value by over $100,000 due to appreciation alone. The buyer didn't do anything to the property. He decided to put it right back on the market and sold it for approximately $80,000 in profit without ever having to do anything to his property.

In markets like that, everyone is a superstar. Yet, it's the most dangerous way to get into real estate investing. The flips you see on TV, where they purchase a property that is often dated and or small, renovate or add to it and sell for a profit, involve playing the market and is very risky. You can only hope that you didn't buy in the height of the market and won't have to sell at the bottom. I have seen that, and it is painful and gut wrenching to watch.

The problem with most flippers is that the cycle is tough to break. In Ontario, there is increased competition in this market, and that ultimately leads to margins being driven down and profits suffering as a result. The profit that someone typically makes on a flip in Ontario is no less than 10% of the repair value, at least, that is the margin professional flippers in Southern Ontario look to make when all is said and done. The lower the final selling price of the home, the less the profit. The more expensive the home, the bigger the potential profit, but this comes with a bigger risk too. For example, say someone purchases a house for $350,000, renovates, and sells within a couple of months for $500,000. They are most likely making a profit of roughly $50,000 if everything goes as planned (10% of $500,000—the repair value). The flipper has to take into consideration carrying costs, land transfer cost, renovations costs, miscellaneous and unexpected costs, legal fees, and commissions to pay a Realtor to sell. There's very little room for error when flipping.

Are you fit to flip?

If someone is going to lose money in real estate, there is a good chance that this is where it is going to happen—flipping homes. If the person doesn't already have a network of contractors going into the project, things can get squirrely quickly. Contractor quotes may come in too high, and contracts between the buyer and contractors may have not been written correctly, or even at all. Contractors might run off with large deposits or not maintain the timeline, work might not be done properly, you might run into unforeseen construction and carrying costs not budgeted for, and a multitude of other things can pop up.

Getting a construction manager, also called a general contractor or project manager, can help alleviate a bit of stress on a flip. The construction manager takes care and oversees one of the hardest parts of renovating a property, and that is scheduling of contractors. You don't want to put flooring down before you paint and get paint on your new flooring. Sometimes the plumbers have to get their work done before the electricians come in, and both the plumbers and the electricians definitely need to get in before the people doing drywall come in. But during the framing, plumbing, and electrical work, the city inspector has to come in at various stages to pass the work before the drywall goes up. Renovations need to happen in specific order, and a good construction manager schedules all the trades and inspections in a very specific order according to a specific time frame. Poor scheduling, like waiting for the electricians to finish and then all of a sudden trying to get someone scheduled for drywall, can eat up several more days, weeks, or even a month, depending how booked up these contractors are. Time is of the essence when flipping properties, and every day counts.

Flipping a house for profit takes a lot of time. You'll be picking finishes and if managing the project yourself, you will be managing workers and timelines and need to check in on the progress frequently.

Even if everything goes well on your first flip, you'll need to search weeks or months before you find another home worth flipping, and then you have to go through the time and work of another project before you see a pay cheque again. It's challenging to achieve a reliable source of income when flipping.

As a society, too many people are focused on short-term instant gratification and unrealistic expectations from TV and social media. Needing to build up a nest egg so that one can purchase multiple buy and hold properties is one thing, but flipping to 'get rich quick' is not going to happen in Ontario. For some flippers, short-term goals can often become long-term problems. They would have done much better holding on to a few properties. Just one property alone can change someone's life; you don't need a ton of properties.

To achieve true wealth and success as a real estate investor, you have to commit to the long game. There are much easier ways to do this than flipping properties.

BRRRR strategy

As a Canadian, BRRRR has always meant 'it's freezing!' to me. However, someone recently decided to make BRRRR an acronym for a real estate investing strategy that has been going on for decades. The BRRRR acronym stands for 'buy' a property, 'rehab'(renovate), 'refinance' (pull your equity out), and then 'repeat' (do this strategy again).

The goal is to purchase a property, renovate that property, and then pull out all of the money you put into it when you refinance it. Essentially, you will have purchased the property for nothing out of pocket but still have 20% built-in equity in the home (your initial down payment). Pulling equity from a rental property and using those funds to purchase another property is a pretty popular strategy for investors. The BRRRR strategy can just mean that you are pulling out money more quickly compared to waiting a few years for the mortgage to be paid down and the property to appreciate before you refinance it and tap into that equity. This strategy is used by investors to help acquire and build a portfolio of passive income rental properties without having to continually save up for a new down payment for each investment property they purchase. It's a great strategy to buy multiple properties when you do not have a lot of cash available.

Although the acronym 'BRRRR' is new, the strategy itself has been around for years. Buy a property and put some work into it by updating and improving it, which raises the value of the home. The same thing can be done with your primary residence as well. In this case, you can just skip the 'rent' step of BRRRR. You own your house, you renovate and increase the value, then you refinance drawing on the equity you've built in the home and use that money to buy yourself an investment property.

Here's how the BRRRR strategy works:

Buy

Buy a property that you can add value to through making renovations. For example, you could purchase a single-family home and increase the value of the home through renovations. You can also raise the value of the home by creating a second suite or converting the property to a student rental.

Renovate

You want a home that will increase in value from a renovation (good after-repair value). You also want to renovate the property in such a way that it will bring in maximum rental income once you complete the renovation and find tenants. This helps with cash flow and the appraisal value when you need to refinance the property.

Rent

The property is then advertised for rent, and tenants are screened and selected.

Refinance

Once the renovations have been completed, tenants have signed a lease and are living in your property, it is time to call the bank and tell them you want to refinance the property. The bank will order an appraiser to visit the property and determine its new value. The higher the appraiser values the property, the greater amount of equity you will be able to pull from the property. You're looking to take most of your equity out of the property so that you end up getting all your renovation money back and possibly more and use that money towards your next property.

Repeat

If you are able to pull off the BRRRR strategy well, you should have a cash-flowing property or properties for little to no money invested in the properties. In a perfect world—a fantastic renovation was done on your property, the real estate market continued appreciating aggressively while you were doing your renovations, and the appraiser was generous the day of appraisal—you can pull all your capital back out (your original down payment and your renovations cost) and own this property for zero out of pocket. You can then use all of that money for your next property purchase. You're literally using one property to purchase another; no extra money is coming out of your pocket.

The BRRRR strategy is useful for an investor who wants to amass a decent size portfolio without having to continually save up for a down payment for each investment property. However, like anything in life, this strategy doesn't come without risks. Again, this is where using a reputable renovation contracting team becomes priceless. Working with the wrong contractors can potentially lead to them not maintaining the timeline and work not being done properly. Issues may come up that were not originally budgeted for. An investor needs to go into BRRRR hoping for the best but also planning for the worst. Everything could be going along great, and then a simple thing like an appraisal coming in too low can make a difference of tens of thousands of dollars that you won't have access to for your next property. It will all work out in the long-term, but it has the potential to slow down your next purchase if things do not go as planned.

If you already own a rental property or even your primary residence where you live, odds are you already have built-up equity in your property. The rate that equity accumulates is through appreciation and mortgage paydown. An appraisal is the first step to determine how much equity you can tap into and potentially use to purchase a rental property.

Condos

For an investor who is looking to park their money in real estate, wants little to no maintenance or repair calls, and is willing to make a little less of a return on their money, a condo unit might be a great investment option. Condo units are typically purchased by investors for convenience. A condo unit is typically in a secure building. There is no grass cutting or snow removal, and maintenance and repairs of the building are taken care of through the monthly maintenance fee. The monthly maintenance fee is most often determined as a cost per square foot of the condo unit. If the building is brand new, the monthly maintenance fees typically start at approximately 50 cents per square foot. That means that if you have a 600 sq. ft. condo unit, the monthly maintenance fee will be $300 per month.

Depending on the condo, condo maintenance fees typically cover the expenses for concierge, window and building cleaners, snow and garbage removal, grass cutting, and maintenance and repair of the building itself. Owners don't have to worry about coming up with money to replace a roof, windows, furnace, or AC; everything is covered in the maintenance fee. These fees also take care of maintaining the amenities within the building, such as a gym, rooftop deck, guest suites, meeting rooms, a theatre, dog wash or car wash area, and an indoor or outdoor pool. Generally, the more amenities that a building offers, the higher the monthly maintenance fee.

Condos can be attractive investments

Condos definitely have a different dynamic than single-family homes. Formerly, individuals who chose condo living were people who were single, couples without children, or empty nesters. Nowadays, condo units are becoming the new starter home for many young couples and families because they are cheaper to rent or purchase than a single-family home. This makes for a greater rental pool for this emerging market trend.

Condos are most often located in areas where single-family homes are in short supply. For example, many downtown areas across Southern Ontario are bursting with condos and condo development, while fewer and fewer freestanding residential properties are becoming available. In many downtown locations where once was a parking lot, two-storey home or a row of homes, builders are coming in, purchasing those lots or properties, and then erecting large condo residences. The Ontario provincial legislation has created rules that mandate more density in communities across Southern Ontario, which is leading to fewer and fewer freestanding residential buildings being built. Density is no longer just a big-city issue. This is happening right across Southern Ontario.

If an investor has purchased a condo in the last couple of years anywhere across Southern Ontario, there is likely no positive cash flow being created. These investors often rely on the mortgage being paid down from the rental income and appreciation over time. I know some investors purchase preconstruction condo units on speculation, hoping that when the condo construction is finished and they take possession their unit will be worth more than they paid three, four, five years earlier when they purchased off plans. This is a gamble for sure, and I would never suggest someone purchase a condo unit solely relying on appreciation. There are some factors that can lead to a condo building having a better chance of appreciating than others, but it is never guaranteed. If you can invest in areas where the unit cost per square foot is less than the resale market for a similar condo with a similar size unit in the area, that's generally the first good sign. The amenities of the building, the area, and transit also need to be taken into consideration. This is more than just being on the lookout for a new Starbucks in the area, commonly referred to as the Starbucks Effect. There should be other indicators that a neighbourhood is up-and-coming. A good development is often within close walking distance to a subway station, light rapid transit, or GO transit. If downtown, it should be in close proximity to employers so that residents have the option of cycling or walking to work rather than commuting through downtown traffic. Purchasing in an area that is being established with major amenities, growing in popularity, or going through gentrification is also a good criterion when choosing a condo that you are hoping will appreciate overtime.

Not all condos have to be purchased with the intent on appreciation. Some investors purchase a unit with the intention of renting it out for now but potentially moving into it themselves or letting their children move into it one day. Buying in advance secures them a unit in the area they want to own in while having a tenant pay down their mortgage.

The main disadvantage of buying a condo is that they don't usually cash flow with the typical 20% down payment requirement for an investment property. They also haven't historically appreciated as well as freehold single-family homes. But there are pros and cons to every type of investment. In this case, literally no maintenance calls or repairs but less return on your money and slower appreciation growth. For some investors, the pros might outweigh the cons.

If you're buying a new condo, the key is to get in as early as possible. In order to get the financing to start a new project, builders will often raise initial funding through pre-sales. The pre-sales events usually start off with sales to 'friends and family', and the builder will also open sales to a hand-selected group of 'platinum access Realtors'. Platinum access is incredibly difficult to get with builders. Realtors that get this access are typically bringing in buyers that, in total, are purchasing 20 or more units. That's a good number of sales for the builder. The builder and sales center team for the building prefer these types of sales because they only have to deal with one Realtor for 20 to 30 sales versus having to deal with 30 different Realtors for 30 different buyers. Since we are in the niche business of investment real estate and work with hundreds of investors, we have been able to establish platinum access status with most builders across Southern Ontario. This access provides buyers we work with the opportunity to purchase a condo unit for the lowest price it will be offered. These buyers also get first choice of their unit and floor level. Furthermore, it's the best opportunity to get any incentives the builder may be offering, such as upgraded finishes or free parking and lockers. After the friends and family and platinum access, the builders will continue sales with invitation-only VIP events. It's easy to get in on these VIP pre-sales, but many of the best units will already have been selected. For every platinum access Realtor there are probably 100 other Realtors getting VIP access. You probably also get those 'VIP access' emails if you have ever been in the market for a condo yourself. As the sales open up to the general public and all other Realtors, the prices go up and the incentives get clawed back by the builders. If the condo project is a highly sought-after project, the best inventory typically never hits the open market. This has happened with us with many projects in Southern Ontario. Some of our most recent projects that we had platinum access to, giving investors working with us first choices of units, were such developments as: Daniels Erin Mills—Mississauga, Artistry—Toronto, 55 Mercer—Toronto, Friday Harbour—Innisfil, Television City—Hamilton, Lakeside Residences—Toronto, Galleria—Toronto, and District Trailside—Oakville. Some of these developments are currently under construction. The other builds completed that investors and buyers took possession on already have been very successful purchases.

Artistry in Toronto was our latest condo project that we had platinum access to. Ninety percent of the units were sold out during the friends and family and platinum access. Realtors with VIP access and the general public were left choosing from the 10% of the units that the other 90% of buyers passed on. You can quite easily see the value of working with a Realtor team that has platinum access so that you can get in at the ground level, paying the lowest price and having the luxury of choosing from several different units rather than what is left over.

Importance of a status certificate

When purchasing a resale condo unit, it is incredibly important to request the status certificate of the building and have it reviewed by a lawyer before the purchase goes firm. The lawyer will be looking at key aspects like how well the condo is being managed and how much money is in its reserve fund. Are there are any immediate or near-future expenditures that might require a special assessment and raise the monthly condo fee for all residents? Are there condo rules or restrictions that could conflict with the reason you purchased or with the lifestyle you're seeking in a condo community? For example, some condos forbid leasing to tenants, including short-term rentals and Airbnb. Some also have pet restrictions based on the type and size of the pet.

I know a lady who once attended the sales center of a builder who was selling condo units. She decided to purchase a preconstruction unit. While waiting for the condo to be built, she bought a puppy. A few years later the condo was ready for her to finally move in. A few weeks after moving in she received a letter from the condo board stating she had to get rid of her dog because the breed was in violation of the condo rules and regulations! I think any dog owner would sympathize with her. She didn't want to get rid of her dog, and after multiple threats from the builder's lawyer she had to do something she didn't want to do; she sold her unit and moved out. This proves how important it is to review an up-to-date status certificate so that you don't become the bearer of any costly increases in the maintenance fee or fall victim to a lifestyle restriction from the condo board.

Conclusion

When it comes to investing, a condo can be a great hands-off approach for an investor. The cash flow will most likely be nonexistent or negative, but you'll enjoy ease of management and repairs being taken care of by the maintenance fees. It all depends on your short-term objectives and long-term goals, your financial situation, and your target renters.

What makes a good investment property?

It's better to miss a good one than buy a bad one

It's important that you don't stumble out of the gates when purchasing an investment property. Picking the wrong property will hurt a lot more than your bank account. The wrong purchase can be financially and mentally disastrous. Mentally you'll be beat down, you probably will never invest in real estate again, and you are likely to vent to your significant other or friends about your bad experience, unjustly turning them off real estate too.

The information I provide in this book is intended as a guide to help you further conduct your analysis before purchasing an investment property. Once you better equip yourself with this knowledge, I truly believe you will see how valuable it is to work with a Realtor who works specifically in the niche of investment real estate and has a proven track record, not only for themselves but for their clients as well.

My team and I see this as much more than doing 'a deal'. If an investor wants to purchase a property that we don't believe is a good investment, we simply will not do the deal. That's right! We will gladly pass up the commission on a purchase or sale if we ourselves don't believe in the investment. Assisting an investor to purchase the wrong property becomes our problem as well because not only do we help investors find properties, we also help them fill and manage their properties if they so desire. Their headache becomes our headache, and selfishly, we don't want any headaches. My team and I are licensed Realtors yes, but that is only because we are real estate investors first. Every single person on my team, including myself, were real estate investors first. We were purchasing properties ourselves. Once I saw how lucrative real estate investing was, I went out and got my real estate license, which gave me access to real estate boards, information and history on properties, and the ability to view and get into these properties. We are not like the Realtors that you see on TV saying, "Look at these nice oak cabinets and beautiful granite counter tops..." We guide the investor through everything and give them all the information you need: What price you can pick the property up for, how much it will rent for, what your cash flow will be, what type of tenant you are going to get, how long it will take before your property is filled with a tenant, the amenities in the area, why a tenant would want the place, etc. If the property is no good, we will let the investor know so that we can move on and find a property that is good rather than letting the investor make a bad buying decision. Our investors rely on our expertise. They are leaning on us for information and decision-making. If we wouldn't buy the property ourselves, we are not going to suggest that another investor buy it.

We look for properties daily for investors that we work with. We have four full-time staff, myself and three team members, who are on the streets daily going through properties all across Southern Ontario. Every day we view single- and multi-family homes, student rentals, possible conversions, new developments...and much more. Needless to say, we each put a ton of kilometers on our cars. We also have a dedicated, full-time assistant in our office who is constantly on the computer searching for properties that get listed on the Realtor boards. She knows which city each team member is in at any time and calls one of us the minute a new listing comes up that may be a great investment opportunity. Every week we also have regular meetings with builders, property managers, private sellers, and contractors so that we have the best opportunity to get great investment properties for the investors that we are so fortunate to work with.

What makes our daily search of properties so interesting is the dynamics of the real estate landscape. There is a myriad of factors to look at when it comes to selecting investment properties.

Once we find a property that we feel is a good investment, we inform the investor and explain all the details and why it is a good property. We discuss the physical characteristics of the property, the location, the projected income, expenses, and returns, and our executive assistant sends the listing and photos to the investor. There are thousands of properties listed for sale at any given time across Southern Ontario, but only a small handful will make the cut as a great investment property.

We also look for hidden value-adds to these investment properties. Can we turn a single-family home into a great second suite or student rental to increase cash flow? Is the property on a large lot where we can sever and build a second property or sell off that severed piece of land for additional income?

We also have access to off-market deals from sellers who don't want to list on MLS for various reasons, for example in the case of a divorce where some discretion is required. Sellers might also not want a bunch of strangers trekking through their open house or nosey neighbours coming through just to see what their own house could sell for. Some people need to sell very fast to a qualified buyer, and a good portion of the general public knows that we work with investors who can close on a transaction literally within a couple weeks.

How we grade properties

When looking at properties with investors, we go through each property while physically taking notes. Once we finish looking at all the properties available that day, we grade each property with an A, B, C, D, or F, with a + or –, much like how we were graded in school.

The grading is predicated on many factors; location, price, neighbours, amenities, layout of the home, room sizes, numbers of bedrooms and bathrooms, updates to the home, and the majors: condition and age of plumbing, electrical, furnace, AC, roof, and windows. We also consider the condition of and type of foundation, available parking, visitor parking, public transportation, and schools in the area.

Grade A

A Grade A property has a great location with many amenities and great schools in the area. The house is either a young home with no foreseeable maintenance coming down the road, or all the majors have been updated: roof, furnace, AC, windows, electrical, etc. If it is an older home, the interior of the property is updated. It has a garage, two full bathrooms, three or more bedrooms, finished basement, large lot, double-wide drive, and visitor parking. It is close to public transportation (but not right outside the front door), will rent fast, and for top dollar. It is close to highways and arterial roads, retail and grocery shopping, medical services, entertainment, and other sought-after amenities. These are the types of homes where you can typically see yourself living there. They are 100% turnkey properties. They are the homes where an investor purchases the property, closes on it, fills it, and moves on to the next property.

A Grade A property doesn't have to be brand-new. More often than not, in Southern Ontario, these are not new properties. Desirable locations are already built up with homes and are established neighbourhoods with all major amenities in close proximity. That's what makes the location so great.

Demand for this type of property will always exceed supply, therefore these areas tend to be the benefactors of strong appreciation growth. Grade A properties are the hardest to find, but patient, persistent investors will be very grateful once they have one. These properties rent fast, re-rent fast, and sell fast. They carry the highest price tag. You may not cash flow on this type of property because of the higher price paid, but you will have fewer headaches and foreseen expenses due to the fact that the property is updated and the rental market is extremely strong. If priced right, these are often tough properties to negotiate on because of the demand sellers will get from buyers.

Grade B

A Grade B property is still a great investment option but doesn't quite have the full features of an A property. Maybe it has one full bathroom instead of two. Maybe it has parking for two cars but not a double-wide driveway. Maybe it requires a few minor updates, etc.

The great thing about Grade B properties is that often, with a little extra cash, we can turn the property into an A property. For example, we could add the extra full bathroom, finish the basement, or widen the driveway. Other things we may not be able to change, so it will always be a B type property, for example if it is in a B location, such as backing onto an apartment building, on a bit of busy street, or there's a stop sign directly outside the front of the house.

Nevertheless, B's are often the best classification to purchase. There are more of these types of properties available compared to Grade A properties. As a result, there will be slightly less competition from buyers, and therefore you may be able to negotiate on the purchase price.

Grade C or D

Grade C or D properties are iffy purchases. Usually we pass on these unless the investor wants to do extensive renovations or is a contractor. First, we look at the listing online to see whether the property is worth checking out. Walking through a property and looking at it online are two completely different things. If you ever tried online dating you can relate! We usually know going to view these properties that they are going to be questionable, but we never want to miss a diamond in the rough. Just like some good photos of a property can make the property look better than it is, there can also be bad photos of a good property.

Once we physically go through one of these properties, we typically realize that there is quite a bit of work to do before the property can be offered up as a good rental property. These types of properties may have the 50- to 60-year-old kitchen and bathrooms. Often, a few of the big-ticket items need replacing as well, for example the furnace, AC, roof, or windows. The property might be powered by fuses instead of breakers.

There will definitely be less competition for buyers in the C category. You could potentially get a deal, but you need to be prepared for renovation costs and work. Here you can definitely negotiate the price of the property. For an investor who wants to do some work— renovation, conversion, or flip—such an investment could be a decent opportunity, but for the average investor who just wants to purchase a property and rent it out, A or B Grade properties is the way to go.

With D properties, you are likely setting yourself up to fail. When you go to view these properties you usually quickly realize why the Realtor only chose exterior photos of the house and no interior photos. Maybe the Realtor only included a couple of the 'good' interior photos, leaving the rest to your imagination. These properties are typically money pits in need of many updates and repairs, often repairs that just don't make financial sense for an investor, for example a low basement ceiling, leaking block foundation, mold, all majors needing replacement, water-damaged ceilings, old electrical, and old appliances. Often there is literally nothing to salvage except for the structure. D properties are usually best for professional flippers that need a project to keep their crews busy at the expense of making very minimal profit.

F

An F Grade property is a complete bust. We usually end up physically running out of these properties. An F Grade property usually meets all the criteria of a D property but with even bigger problems: the integrity of the property's foundation or structure has been compromised, all majors need to be replaced, there is extensive water damage, knob and tube electrical wiring, vermiculite in the attic, asbestos, UFFI, undesirable next-door neighbours, mold, the property is on a flood plain, hard to insure, smells of smoke and fecal matter…oh yes, these properties exist and are bad.

If I wouldn't personally buy it, I wouldn't recommend that you purchase it either, and this is usually the case with an F Grade property.

CHAPTER 5

Coming Up with The Money To Purchase an Investment Property

If you are not in the financial position you'd like to be, it is not because of a shortage of opportunity!

There are multiple options for investors to qualify and purchase rental properties. After we have our initial meeting with an investor and get a better understanding of their short-term objectives and long-term goals, we provide them with access to a lender. The lender sits down with the investor and explains a strategy that best fits that particular client's short-term objectives and long-term goals. Going to your bank to get qualified for a mortgage for an investment property is definitely not the only route a buyer should consider when looking for a pre-approval for a mortgage.

There are many financing options available: mortgage brokers, A-lenders, B-lenders, credit unions, private lenders, and joint venture partners. There are a wide range of terms and conditions that apply to these loans because of the various mortgage and lending options available to you. The most common is for a lender to allow you to borrow 80% of the value of the property, which would be amortized over 25 to 30 years. However, with private lending and joint ventures, it's possible to purchase a property for zero money out of pocket instead of paying a 20% down payment.

As investors, we just don't want to choose the lender that can get us the lowest interest rate. We always ask ourselves, can this particular lender get us multiple mortgages, and if so, how many? Will this affect us when we try to qualify with another lender after we have maxed out how many mortgages this one particular lender can provide for us? There's a strategy behind getting as many mortgages as you can, and this is why I personally work with the top mortgage broker in Canada versus using my own bank of over 30 years.

The first job of the lender that you choose to use is to get you a 'pre-approval' that provides you with the details of how much of a property you can afford and how much of a down payment you will need to come up with. The lender will also advise you on where that down payment should best come from, i.e. RRSP, savings, a line of credit, a gift, refinancing a mortgage, or maybe a home equity line of credit.

Here are the most common ways for a purchaser to come up with the down payment for the purchase of a rental property.

HELOC

If you are presently a homeowner and have owned your home for quite some time, you have likely benefited from appreciation on your property and mortgage balance paydown from the monthly mortgage payments you have been making. If you currently have a mortgage on your home, you may very well have hundreds of thousands of dollars in equity that you can tap into to purchase rental properties. The two methods typically used to gain access to the increased equity in one's home are through refinancing or a home equity line of credit (HELOC).

A HELOC is considered one of the most popular ways to borrow money as a down payment for the purchase of an investment property. This method involves taking out a home equity line of credit on a property that has decent equity built up. Many investors prefer this method because the cost of this type of borrowing is typically one of the cheapest ways to get access to cash if you don't have decent savings readily available in the bank. This form of lending is also flexible. If you have a lot of equity in your home, you can borrow that money and have it working for you instead of it just sitting there untouched not making you any money.

A home equity loan can equal as much as 80% of the value of your home. Let's assume that you have a home today that is worth $500,000, and the balance of a mortgage of $100,000. The bank will calculate 20% of $500,000, which is $400,000, minus the $100,000 existing mortgage. Now you have access, at any time, to up to $300,000. This comes as a line of credit you can withdraw from as needed. During this time, the borrower pays interest on the credit balance and does not have to pay any money towards the principal each month. As an investor, there are also tax advantages to this approach.

Many investors use a HELOC to provide for the initial down payment when they purchase an investment property. Some investors may further use a HELOC to cover the renovation costs of a property they just purchased. The investor can use the money to update the property or possibly cover the cost of a conversion to a legal second suite property. After renovations are completed, they can then refinance to pull the cash back out of the renovated property and pay off their HELOC balance. They then have the option of doing this all over again. This is also referred to as the BRRRR strategy as discussed in Chapter 4.

It's hard to beat this kind of deal that gives you a ready source of cash and opens the door for you to start investing in properties. You can literally acquire investment properties with zero to little cash out of pocket.

Refinancing

Refinancing is basically the process of getting a new mortgage by renegotiating and technically paying off your existing home mortgage. This creates a new mortgage on your home that replaces the one that is presently on it. You would literally receive the money as a lump sum payment sitting in your bank account, ready to use for a property purchase.

Refinancing can help with paying off other debt if needed, taking advantage of lower interest rates, and getting access to cash to use towards the down payment of a rental property. Investors who already have a few rental properties can look at refinancing any of their existing rental properties instead of tapping into their personal home equity. If the tenants have been paying down the mortgage and the property has been appreciating over time, the investor can leverage that equity to purchase their next investment property, often with no money out of their own pocket.

A-lenders

'A-lenders' is the term given to traditional lenders like our big five banks: Scotia, RBC, CIBC, Bank of Montreal, and TD. These lenders like to focus on buyers who have good credit scores and a reliable source of income. The term A-lender comes from the fact that the buyers they work with are top-tier 'A' clients

If you are considered an 'A' client with your bank, they may have already given you a pre-approval to go out and purchase another property. However, keep in mind that this may come back to bite you in the butt one day. Best to always consult a top-of-the-field lender if you are considering purchasing an investment property. One wrong loan can offset your debt-to-service ratios so badly that trying to get a third or fourth mortgage approval could be almost impossible.

B-lenders

"B-lenders" and credit unions are institutions that offer options for a buyer who would be considered a "B" client. A 'B' client's application typically shows something that doesn't meet the qualifying criteria of an 'A-lender'. Clients needing to use a 'B-lender' or credit union typically lack the desired credit score, or they don't meet the source of income requirement of 'A-lenders'. Sometimes 'B' lenders work well for self-employed individuals.

Essentially, these institutions offer a lower barrier of entry to qualify than an 'A-lender', but these approvals are often offset with higher interest rates on loans.

Joint venture

If down payment or qualifying is an issue for an investor, a joint venture may very well be a great alternative to get them into the market.

There are so many ways to do a joint venture. I will describe the most common joint venture partnership to not complicate how this type of investment generally works. Often the catalyst for a joint venture is a scenario where there is an individual who wants to invest in an income property. They can't qualify for a mortgage on their own, so they need a partner to step in and qualify for a mortgage on their behalf. Often the person looking for a joint venture partner is also someone looking for an equity partner. They need a partner who can come up with a down payment and qualify for the mortgage. The person qualifying for the mortgage is the equity partner. The other partner is the sweat equity partner. The sweat equity partner typically finds the property, fills the property with tenants, and property manages the property for as long as these partners own the property together. The typical split on profit for a joint venture arrangement between two such partners is 50/50 on all income and expenses.

The partner that puts up the equity and qualifies for the mortgage is typically someone who has access to good equity but is busy with their careers, families, or hobbies. Sometimes the equity partner can even be someone who is retired and looking for extra cash flow and investments in their life. They might want to have a rental property but don't have the time to look at properties and fill and manage tenants.

In return for putting up the money for the down payment and qualifying for the mortgage, the equity partner takes 50% of the return on the investment. The benefit for this partner is that they get in on a rental property and they never need to view properties nor ever take a tenant or maintenance call.

The sweat equity partner gets the other 50% return on the investment because they are the one doing all the work; finding the property, filling the property with a tenant, dealing with any updates or repairs to the property, and refilling the property with new tenants when the time comes.

Joint venture partners need to sign a joint venture agreement that lays out the details of the partnership, i.e. who is responsible for what, the percentage share each party gets, and most importantly, the terms of dissolvement of the agreement. There may come a time when one partner wants to sell the property and get their share of the profit, while the other wants to keep the property. Will one partner buy the other one out? If so, for how much? Or will the property just go up for sale on the market and both partners cash out? The terms of the dissolvement of the partnership should be agreed upon before closing on a property to avoid displeasure between the parties when one of the partners wants out of the agreement.

The best joint venture partners are typically people who you already know, trust, and have a good relationship with. They can be parents, siblings, aunts, uncles, friends, coworkers, and grandparents.

Private lenders

Private lenders are usually used as a last resort option for buyers. They often require very little in the way of qualification, and as a result, their mortgage rates will be higher than the rates of A- or B-lenders and credit unions. Their rates are usually in the ballpark of 8% to 12%. Private lending is usually unregulated lending, so a lawyer should be consulted to review the documents before signing to make sure the buyer is not entering into unforeseen risk.

Conclusion

Real estate investors have plenty of options to raise the down payment and qualify for a mortgage to purchase an investment property. It's great to be creative, but we must also not over-leverage ourselves. Deciding whom to consult with and use for your down payment may feel daunting.

When we learn our investors' short-term objectives and long-term goals, we have a very good idea of what type of lender they should approach and how. We provide our investors with lenders that specialize in investment properties. These lenders are there to get the investors as many properties as possible with the least money out of pocket and at the lowest interest rates available. They clearly understand investment mortgages.

Not choosing the right lender can cost you tens of thousands of dollars in higher interest rate payments and lower monthly cash flow. It can cost you significantly if, when you sell the property, you are forced to pay an excessive penalty to break the existing mortgage—a mortgage that wasn't set up correctly in the first place. It can also stop you from prematurely growing your portfolio of investment properties because you didn't use the banks that are real estate investor friendly.

Banks change their rules all the time. Some banks have caps on how many rental properties we can have mortgages on with their particular bank. Others have caps on how many mortgages you have in total, regardless of what financial institution you have your investment properties with. Not knowing the intricacies of these banks and their limits or which lenders to use in what particular order is often what makes the difference between someone qualifying for a maximum of five properties while others qualify for and own 25 properties or more.

Ultimately, whatever form of financing approval we get as investors, we don't want to leverage ourselves too high, where we are constantly refinancing properties and tapping into every dollar of equity we gain. We never know what's around the corner, and circumstances can change rapidly. We should always leave ourselves a strong buffer of finances and unused credit that we can access quickly and easily if ever needed. Having a strong network with a real estate specific lender should help keep these checks and balances in place.

<u>CHAPTER 6</u>

The Five Biggest Mistakes a New Investor Can Make and How to Avoid Them

Most people prefer a good excuse to a good opportunity!

Trying to time the market

Did you hear about the fortune teller that won the lottery? Neither have I. It has never happened, for real, you can Google it. Some hopeful investors want to invest in real estate but say they'll do it when the market hits rock bottom. Nobody can time the top, middle, or bottom of the market. It's never clear in real time. Everything seems to make sense and be logical in retrospect. We can only make sense of the markets looking back after a few months or likely a few years later, because the real estate market, although volatile, is not as volatile as other markets like stocks that swing up and down in price daily, almost second by second.

Whether we are a regular home buyer or investor, we are typically purchasing a property without knowing exactly what market we are in. Even if we happen to be purchasing a property that is at the bottom of the market at that time, we have no way of knowing that prices won't go down further. The same goes for when property prices are going up. We can never tell if we are purchasing at the top of the market for the same reason. The property we are purchasing might be more expensive than it ever has been, but how can we certain at that moment in time that prices won't continue going up? We can't. We will only know if we bought at the top of the market or at the bottom of the market years down the road.

For those waiting for real estate prices to drop in Southern Ontario, it is 100% possible that they will see properties go down, even a couple of times. Those who are waiting for prices to drop will have their dream come true eventually. There's only one small problem with this. When prices of properties in strong areas such as Southern Ontario go down in price, there is usually a much bigger global crisis happening, such as the global financial crisis of 2008. At a time like this, lenders usually freeze up lending. Would-be buyers are not usually sitting on large sums of cash, particularly in times of crises. They wouldn't be able to purchase a property because banks would be protecting their risk of losses in a market correction.

Property prices would eventually rise and rebound, banks would start lending again, and the buyer who was trying to purchase at the bottom of the market but couldn't would now most likely say they missed their chance and they will wait for the next market correction. This is like a dog chasing its tail.

Knowing we can never tell what market we are in is the number-one reason we like starter homes on the outskirts of the Greater Toronto area. In 2008, with the world financial crisis and in 2017, with stress-test lending and foreign buyer tax, some housing prices were definitely affected. Those homes that experienced a price drop was in the category of luxury real estate in the Greater Toronto Area and Southern Ontario. Many luxury homes were selling for 20% less, hundreds of thousands of dollars, than they would have sold for a few months earlier. The property prices that did not come down during these times were starter home properties in the $400,000 to $500,000 range.

In turbulent economic times like these, news headlines and reports like to blanket the real estate market with one broad heading, such as "Property prices in Ontario fall by 20%." The problem with this is that it is incredibly vague. Some property prices definitely fell by 20% during those times. Other properties, like starter homes, were still selling at or above the price they sold for before these market corrections. The general public doesn't interpret the news that way unfortunately, and those types of headlines can make buyers fearful and potentially miss a great buying opportunity.

We are currently in the second month of the Covid-19 pandemic and have yet to see what will happen to home prices across Ontario. Even if real estate prices do come down for a bit as a result of people losing their jobs and businesses going bankrupt, the luxury real estate market will typically be the one that takes the brunt of the correction. That's not to say that the starter home market won't come down in price too; it's just that this particular segment of the market tends to have a much softer landing during turbulent markets.

The reality is, in good times or bad, we all need food, water, and shelter. During a financial crisis, families are even more likely to tighten down on their discretionary spending and not purchase that big luxury home they wanted. They would rather play it safe and purchase a starter home, while others might downsize from big homes into smaller homes. These moves continue to put pressure and demand on the starter home market.

Back in the late 90s, I had people telling me we were in a real estate bubble. I know a couple of people who sold their primary residence and brought their family into a rental property, stating they would purchase when the market corrected. From the late 90s to early 2020, the starter market hasn't 'corrected' yet. That's over 20 years of appreciation and mortgage paydown. If these doomsday sellers still owned their home, it would have probably been paid off by now and they would be mortgage free. The problem is that these 'good times to buy' (bad times economically) have such a long time in between that it may not be worth the wait. 2020 might be their year; we will see. But they definitely won't be buying a home in 2020 for the price they could have purchased one for in the late 90s.

Other comments I hear all the time include things like "property prices just can't keep going up," "housing is unaffordable," "we are in a bubble," "I can't believe housing prices," "I could have bought that for XXXX five years ago." These statements have no substance. This is just someone expressing their feelings, and we really can't make a wise investment decision based on feelings. But if someone were to say, "The government just changed down payment rules so that everyone must put down 20% or more, including first time home buyers," or "Canada is shutting its doors to new immigrants," then that would be big news and a time to maybe wait to see how the market reacts before running out and purchasing a property. In the meantime, we can't control whether we are in a bubble or not. Maybe we are at the top of the market when we purchase or maybe we are somewhere near the middle. Tomorrow will come, time will go on, and if we have a tenant in our property, they are paying down our mortgage regardless of where the market is at. Owning starter homes in good areas that cash flow in times of economic uncertainty allows us to ride out any downward pressure in home prices until the market recovers. Good quality, single-family homes in good areas that pay for themselves are still the easiest piece of real estate to own during any sudden changes to the market.

As long as there is housing, there will always be those people who are waiting for a crash. How long can these people wait? What other investments have they made that have come close to the returns that real estate in Southern Ontario has afforded owners? What are they going to do to make up for lost time? Fear is not rewarded, courage is. News reports, headlines, YouTubers—they can't predict the future, although they pretend to know what is coming next. We can't fall victim to that type of thinking. Nobody knows and nobody ever will know the exact outcome of an investment. The best way to establish a safe investment is by buying cash flow positive real estate and mixing up different types of property investments in a way that reduces risk and maximizes reward.

Not working with a specialized team

Everyone has to start from somewhere. I get it; heck I did, we all did. However, when you are first starting out as a real estate investor you may want to get advice from those that focus on investment real estate day in and day out before rolling the dice with someone who is either new to real estate or doesn't primarily focus on investment real estate themselves.

If the person who is representing you to make one of the most expensive purchases in your life doesn't own real estate investment properties themselves in the city you are looking to invest and they haven't helped many others do the same, how much do they truly know about the market? Do they know the right areas? Do they know the correct value of a property? Market rents? How long it takes to fill a property? Is that particular area more susceptible to an issue like a flood plain, crime, insect or rodent infestation? What are the schools like? Do they know how easy or difficult it is to rent in that area? The renter demographics? The best ways to advertise to tenants? The list goes on.

My team and I have an expanded Rolodex that collectively form an incredible power team. We have all been working together for over a decade. This team consists of home inspectors, mortgage brokers, lawyers, property managers, contractors, paralegals, accountants, architects, developers, and much more.

Real estate is pretty safe bet. It can often be the people that make it risky; buyers getting the wrong advice on a property, landlords or property managers not choosing the right tenants. As an investor, you need to choose the right property and have a strong network behind you.

Everyone has opinions. Unless your real estate investment advisor is very experienced, their opinions are often not what you should bet your money on. It's the same as seeking advice in any other area of life or business. Is the person giving you the advice a professional in the field that you are searching for knowledge? Have they created the results for themselves that you are seeking answers for?

I have personally witnessed people lose their life savings after taking the wrong real estate advice. It pains me to meet these people that come to me afterwards and ask for help to get them back to a better position in life. If they had come to me first, I wholeheartedly believe I could have eliminated so much of the loss they endured both financially and emotionally. It's not that I believe anyone is giving bad advice for vindictive reasons. Usually it is just done for profit without the full understanding of the investment. Investing in real estate is hard enough without handicapping yourself straight out of the gates. Investors must work with Realtors who specialize in this very niche market and block out all the other noise.

Losing out on an opportunity

A dead fish almost cost us the deal…

Real estate investing can almost be thought of as business in a box. You come up with a down payment, you purchase a property, you advertise to your customers (tenants), and you generate revenue by collecting rent.

I don't know of a better business than this. You're not paying crazy franchise fees, your profit margins are incredibly high, your product (a home) is not a passing fad, you are not holding inventory that can spoil or be stolen, and you have a ton of customers (tenants).

However, some people continually lose out on opportunities. They have trouble pulling the trigger to purchase a property and it ends up costing them more in the end.

Instead of trying to time the market or negotiate to try and get the lowest price and potentially lose a good opportunity, sometimes it's just better to focus on what you have to pay and how you can make that property bring in more revenue for you. This might include renting the property by the room, dividing it up and creating a second suite, or maybe fixing up the property to rent it out for a higher price. One can even furnish a property and rent it out as a luxury rental.

Still, some people just can't pull the trigger and purchase a property because they look back at the prices that they could've have paid for that property a year or two or 10 years earlier. They say, "This is ridiculous, it's just too expensive!" If people looked at real estate prices the same way they looked at food prices, they would have starved to death by now considering how much more we are paying for groceries compared to five to 10 years ago.

Some of the biggest missed opportunities in real estate is letting self-doubt take over or not offering enough money and missing out on the opportunity. I am 100% not encouraging over-paying for a property here. It's foolish to over-pay for a property, plain and simple. However, trying to nickel and dime a seller over every last cent and potentially losing a great opportunity can cost an investor tens of thousands or hundreds of thousands of dollars in the long-term. I once worked with an investor who almost lost a deal on a property he was purchasing because he demanded to have the seller's wood plaque mounted fish included in the deal...I kid you not. The seller never did end up parting with his trophy fish and the investor still did purchase the property, but it was a close one. And I can assure you the investor is very happy he followed through and purchased the property despite not getting his fish.

In our Southern Ontario market, trying to get a great 'deal' on a property can take a year or two. Look for deals, yes absolutely, don't over-pay, absolutely, but make sure your negotiating is commensurate with the market conditions. In a buyer's market, sellers have a harder time to sell. This is where the buyer has the best opportunity to negotiate and bring the seller down on their selling price. In a seller's market, sellers know they are holding the cards and are often getting their price or a little more, depending on how desirable their property is. It is important to know which market you are purchasing or selling in.

As investors, we need to be careful of stubbornly trying to save $5,000 or $10,000 on a purchase price. If we keep losing out on offers, how much are those same types of properties we missed out on going to sell for four, six, 12 months later? If property prices have gone up $20,000 to $50,000 since we first started looking, we are essentially paying more even if we still get that $10,000 discount we were searching for so desperately.

You can only start generating revenue and leveraging your money once you own a property. If you spend all your time trying to get a deal and don't get a property, you've wasted valuable time not realizing appreciation, mortgage paydowns, and cash flow. The returns of ownership will be much better than the one-off deal where you saved $5,000 or $10,000 on the purchase price. Sometimes we just have to pay what we need to pay.

How many times have you looked back at a home where the price seemed a bit of a stretch initially but in hindsight you know you should have bought it?

The danger of losing out on offers on properties shouldn't be dismissed casually. Depending on market conditions, thousands of dollars can be left on the table for an offer not won. We should negotiate as best we can, and sometimes we may need to check our ego at the door and pay what we need to pay to get a good income-producing asset under our belt.

Getting screwed on a renovation

Our team works with multiple types of contractors across Southern Ontario. We've been working with the majority of them for over a decade. We cherish this group as they are another integral piece of the puzzle towards the success of the investors we work with. Unfortunately, not all contractors are the same. In the beginning, we endured the bumps and bruises of using the wrong contractors, whom we quickly terminated, to finally build a strong network of multiple contractor teams and handymen that we trust and can rely on to this day. Many of the contractors we work with not only do work on our investment properties they also do work on the homes we live in with our families.

Finding good quality, fairly priced, reliable, timely contractors is a real challenge if you don't already have this type of network. Whether you are updating a property, adding a second suite, flipping a property, or just in need of a repair, you really need to choose your contractor wisely. No one ever sets out to hire a bad contractor. We have all heard the stories of subpar contractor work; a contractor who ran off with money, or others who didn't follow the timeline, leaving work uncompleted for months.

If you are in need of a contractor and you don't have a connection to a reputable team, there are several things that can be done upfront to prevent you from getting screwed by a contractor.

Referrals

Ideally, you should start by getting three separate quotes from contractors referred to you by people you know and trust. Arrange that the contractors visit the location at different times (in increments of at least an hour) so that they are not stepping over one another when quoting the project.

Detailed quotes

While collecting quotes, tell each contractor that you have a zero-tolerance policy for projects going over budget. I sometimes feel that inexperienced contactors think that homeowners or investors have so much money that it is not a big deal if they come back with an 'added cost'. I find that when you state upfront that you have zero tolerance for projects going over budget, contractors have no incentive to run costs up and will be very careful with their quote and the work being done.

You don't want to discover that the contractor underbid with his quote to get the job and then get hit with surprise costs midway through the renovation. Surprises can happen, absolutely, but if there is an added cost to the project there needs to be a valid, unforeseen reason for it that a good contractor would not have been able to call out prior to the contract signing. For instance, if you are getting a quote for a basement renovation and there is an obvious sign of some kind of moisture penetration, this should be called out and planned for as a contingency quote for a potential repair that may not be part of the initial agreement. Perhaps there is reason to suspect that the basement is not properly insulated. In this case, there should be a contingency quote to add insulation if necessary, outlining what the cost would be per square foot. If you don't get worst-case scenario (contingency) quotes it would be hard to later prove that a contractor intentionally underbid a project. You'll find that good contractors will have better insights about what may lie beneath the surface and behind the walls of a house. They often also have good ideas for finishing, materials, design, and ways to cut down costs.

Way back in the day, we needed to have a fence installed at a property. At the time, we didn't have our network of contractors fully established yet. We found a couple of contractors through a reputable website and had them come out and quote the project. The contractor we chose asked for a deposit, and I stated that we would do a draw. The agreement was that we would pay a portion once they put in the posts and the remainder once they attached the fence to the posts. While attempting to put in the posts, they used a drill bit that was not suitable for the shale in the ground, and they ended up breaking two drill bits. They never returned after the second one broke. This was an unfortunate situation. We didn't know that particular area had hard shale, and they obviously didn't know either, but it was no money out of our pocket. I guess these guys decided the work would be too much for them, and we never heard from them again. We called another company that was more prepared for this scenario, did the draw with them, and everything worked out perfectly. I will never know how it would have played out if we had given the contractors the deposit they requested. I like to think that I am optimistic, but I am pretty sure they would have said the job is more work than they thought was required and would have asked for more money.

Another time, I coordinated an electrician job in Toronto. We were quoted $1,500 to do some electrical work for a triplex that one of our investors had just purchased. Again, this was way back in the day, over a decade before we established our strong network of contractors. I got three quotes and selected the one in the middle, which looked good. His quote described exactly what was going to be done for the cost of $1,500. At the end of the job, his bill was almost twice the original quote. When I questioned how the final bill almost doubled without us giving him authorization, he stated that the bill included his travel time from his home to the property, there and back. He also added costs (gas and parts) for going to Home Depot twice for parts he didn't have but needed for the job. Since I was the one who coordinated this electrician for the investor, I felt 100% responsible. I told the contractor he wouldn't be paid any more than the original $1,500 that was quoted. Meanwhile, I told the investor what happened. He was ok with paying, but I refused and said I couldn't let him pay out of principle. A week or two later, the electrician came to my place of business and served me with a small claims lawsuit. Months later, the electrician and I attended court. He explained to the judge why he thought his price was justified, and I explained to the judge how the initial quote almost doubled once he threw in all these added costs for his driving and gas. The judge sided with us, and the electrician got his $1,500, which we always agreed to pay, but not the almost $2,500 he wanted. The moral of the story is we need everything in writing. The electrician could've simply said in his original quote that his travel time would be an additional $1,000. To bill us for that amount unexpectedly without prior agreement was not acceptable.

Most contractors are good people. I am not trying to paint a bad picture at all. Just make sure you do your diligence, use a contractor with good references, and make sure every single cost and contingency is accounted for in the quote.

Timeline

Another key item to describe in a renovation contract is time frame of the work. How long is the work going to take? It's just human nature to overestimate what we can do in a day, and contractors are no different. This is often called 'the planning fallacy'—the tendency to underestimate the time that it is going to take to complete a project. The way to best set up and keep the renovation on schedule is to include in writing what shall be done by what date.

Draw schedule

References, detailed written quotes, and a realistic timeline are important considerations when deciding on a contractor. However, there is a fourth crucial part to complete before hiring and signing a contract for renovations, and that is the breakdown of the draw schedule. The draw schedule determines when the owner releases funds to the contractor. Most draw schedules link payments to milestones in the project, such as completion of framing or drywall. Or perhaps once the flooring is in, the owner will pay for the next item to be installed, i.e. a kitchen. Draw schedules can also be linked to the percentage of the job that is completed. In either scenario, the draw (payment) should be roughly equal to the value of the work completed. This way, in the event that a contractor is not performing as expected, it's much easier to agree to terminate the rest of the work, and neither the contractor nor the owner is out of pocket for work not completed. This is where a lot of homeowners mess up. They don't have a draw schedule and pay the contractor a 50% deposit upfront before any work has even started. If that contractor is only a couple days into the job and you are already not happy with the work…you've lost your leverage. The contractor already has 50% of the money. Good luck trying to get money back in this case.

I've definitely done a deposit upfront before. In these cases, it is usually for payment of materials. However, nowadays, we have such a strong network of contractors that, depending on the size of the job, we are only paying at the end of the job once we are satisfied with its completion.

Conclusion

One of the most important skills real estate investors can learn is how to hire and manage contractors, as well as build relationships with them. Unless you're an expert contractor yourself, you'll need to screen contractors properly, get everything in writing, and create a draw schedule to protect your investment.

Once you have established a reliable contracting crew, you can have confidence that your contractor will complete the job satisfactorily, on-schedule, and on-budget, so that you can spend more time on what is important to you and less time screening, hiring, and overseeing contractors and their work. SEP

For larger projects, you always want to use licensed and bonded contractors. This means there's a much better chance that if any damage is done during the renovation or construction, the contractor will take the responsibility for it. Their insurance would also extend to any of their workers if they were to have any injury during construction. You should also look into any rebates that the government may be offering. These rebates often change every few years, depending on which party is in government, but it's always worth checking into. The rebates offered by the Ontario government often apply to upgrading the property's energy efficiency, i.e. installing new windows, doors, insulation, furnace, AC, etc. The rebates can be small incentives of a couple hundred dollars to a couple thousand dollars depending on the work done to the property.

Delaying the eviction process

This chapter is not about the almighty landlord and does not imply in any way that tenants are beneath them; this is far from the truth. If you have ever heard someone say, "It's impossible to get tenants out of a property if they are not paying rent!", or "The Landlord Tenant Board favors tenants!", or "You can't evict someone in the middle of winter!", those statements are simply not true. The Landlord Tenant Board (LTB) is an adjudicative tribunal operated by the Government of Ontario that provides dispute resolution of landlord and tenant matters. It's one of our justice systems that doesn't favor the landlord nor the tenant. The adjudicator hears evidence and makes decisions based on the evidence. A tenant cannot simply stop paying rent and be permitted to remain in a home—our judicial system doesn't allow for that.

As an investor in real estate, there is a chance you might come across a tenant whose behavior or actions force you, as the landlord, to evict your tenant. Hopefully, that never happens to you as a real estate owner, but in case it does, allow me to guide and hopefully provide some comfort to you on how the eviction process currently works in Ontario.

I've personally been through this process only twice in my 20 years of investing. Once for a property that I personally own and the other for a property I helped an investor purchase. And out of the thousands of other properties that I've helped investors with, I'm glad to say that I can't count on more than two hands the amount of times I heard of tenant evictions happening. With good tenant screening and selection, the chances of having to evict are slim, but as property owners, we should know how it works and what actions we must take.

Please note that I am merely outlining the process here. You must always use your judgement and discretion, as every case will be unique and should be handled accordingly. Let's first start with late rent. If rent is not paid by the day after it is due, rent is considered late. Assuming the tenant cannot pay, doesn't have a good excuse for not being able to pay, and is possibly not communicating with the owner, the next step would be to issue an N4 form. The N4, along with instructions to fill it out, can be found on the Ontario government website: www.sjto.gov.on.ca.

I would never personally issue an N4 notice to a tenant on the day after rent is due if that tenant has been making consistent rent payments on time for a year or two. Sometimes, things happen, and the missed payment can be attributed to something simple such as the tenant forgetting it was the first of the month. We really need to use our judgment here, and this is where communication with our tenant is important. In the case of a tenant who has simply stopped paying rent and stopped communicating with the owner or who is continually late with payments, there is help for landlords. These tenants put our financial futures at risk, and we need to act since we are ultimately the ones responsible for the mortgage payments.

There's no cost for issuing the N4. This document informs the tenant that they have 14 days from the day the notice was served to catch up on rent. The landlord must fill out the N4 correctly, otherwise the case can be thrown out. This is when tenants who have stopped paying rent often stay in the house longer than they would have been able to because the landlord didn't fill out the documents correctly in the first place. The N4 is very easy to fill out. There are full instructions on the LTB Government website, and they are only a phone call away for landlord assistance. You must write in your rental property address correctly. If it's an address with units, the unit number must be in there. The tenant's name must be spelled correctly, along with the exact amount of rent that is owed and when it was due.

The N4 serves as the 14 days' notice that rent must be paid. If you provide the notice to the tenant by mail or courier, you have to add extra days in calculating the termination date. If you send the notice by courier, you need to add one business day for delivery. If you are sending the notice by regular mail, you have to add five days for delivery. It is important that you keep a copy of the notice you give the tenants.

If the rent owed is paid prior to the termination date in the notice (the 14 days' notice plus the additional days accounting for delivery), the notice is void and you cannot apply to the LTB to evict the tenant. You are back in good standing, unless rent is late again in the future.

If the tenant does not pay the rent they owe and has not moved out by the termination date, you apply to the LTB for an order to evict the tenant and to collect the rent the tenant owes. The earliest date you can file your application for this hearing with the LTB is the day after the termination date. This process involves filling out a second form, the L1 form. You provide the LTB with your L1 application, the copy of the N4 that you gave to the tenant, and the Certificate of Service that states how and when you gave notice to the tenant.

The LTB then serves the hearing package to both the tenant and the landlord. If at this point, the tenant were to pay all the rent arrears and the filing fee, the eviction would become null and void. If they do not pay or even make a partial payment, the L1 will notify the tenant of the date, time, and location of the hearing, which they will have to attend.

The hearing at the LTB is typically scheduled three to four weeks from the date the hearing package was issued by the LTB. At the hearing, the onus is on the tenant to prove that they have paid rent. As the owner, you should bring the lease and some type of ledger that shows you are keeping track of what rent was paid and what is owed.

At the hearing, you have the option to enter mediations instead of going in front of the adjudicator. In mediations, a neutral mediator attempts to assist the landlord and the tenant to reach an agreement that is acceptable to both sides. Mediation is completely voluntary, and both the landlord and the tenant must agree to mediate for mediation to take place, otherwise the case is heard by the adjudicator. If the landlord and tenant come to an agreement in mediation, the agreement is most often related to a rent repayment schedule. If the tenant does not respect the agreement that was derived from mediation, the landlord might be able to get an eviction order from the LTB without going through the process of getting an N4, L1, and a hearing package.

The eviction is instead expedited. For this reason, the tenant should carefully consider whether they can live up to the conditions of the mediated agreement before they sign it. If the tenant doesn't live up to the conditions, they can be evicted from the home in less than two weeks in some cases.

If the landlord chooses not to go into meditations, the landlord would ask for a 'standard order' when their case is called. A standard order is the right to evict, and if awarded to the landlord, the tenant is usually given 11 days to get out of the house. On the 12th day, if the tenant hasn't paid or hasn't vacated, you place an order with the sheriff. The sheriff will then go to the house and basically tell the tenant they must collect their stuff and get out of the house. A locksmith will change the locks right away so that the tenant no longer has access to the property. If the tenant can't get their personal belongings out of the house right away, they have 72 hours to figure it out. Otherwise, you have the right to remove it. You could take pictures, call a company like 1-800 Got Junk, and have it taken away.

All of this cost a little over $600: the N4 is free, the L1 is $170, the sheriff is $350, and the locksmith is $100. For a little over $600, you get a tenant who is not paying rent out of your property and get your property back. For an extra few hundred dollars, you can also get a paralegal to manage all of this for you on your behalf.

Recouping missing rent after a tenant leaves the house

This is another scenario in which you need to use your own judgement. If a tenant is evicted and the owner is still missing rent, the owner has the option of collecting what is owed by taking the case to the Small Claims Court. The Small Claims Court in Ontario can award losses up to a maximum of $25,000. If you are owed $1,000 to $2,000 as an owner and the tenant has left the house in good standing, you need to weigh out the time and effort it would take to recoup that money. Sometimes I find it is just better to put positive energy back into advertising, showing, and filling the home with a set of new, good tenants. If you put too much effort into trying to recoup a couple thousand dollars, you might be missing the bigger picture. Your main goal should be to get your property show ready again, get it filled, and collect income on it again. However, there will be a dollar threshold where it might make sense to go to Small Claims to collect.

If a landlord wins their case in the Small Claims Court, the best way to typically recoup that money is through wage garnishment. Once their employer receives the garnishment papers, the employer will deduct up to 20% of every paycheck and provide that to the court. If for some odd reason, the garnishee (the employer) doesn't provide the wage garnishment, the owner can proceed with a judgment against the employer.

Overall, the chances of you or someone going to court on your behalf to evict a tenant are quite slim. If anything, a tenant might be a few days late on rent. But more often than not, they make it up quickly, and it ends up being a random occurrence. If it happens too many times, you can issue an N4, and this will usually set them straight. Tenants generally don't want to be evicted. The reality is that if they can't pay your rental, they still need to pay someone else at another property. If they are behind on payments already it would be worse for them to have to come up with the first and last month's rent for a new rental. Also, who would they use as landlord reference? Certainly not you.

CHAPTER 7

What Happens When You Have The Right Network

None of us is as smart as all of us!

- Ken Blanchard

I truly believe that to be successful in whatever endeavor we choose, we must surround ourselves with professionals and people at the top of the field that we are seeking success in. Real estate is no exception. As a real estate investor, we want to have a team of people, our network, around us who have expertise in each element of an investment deal. Andrew Carnegie refers to teamwork as "the fuel that allows common people to attain uncommon results." The most important people in your real estate investing network will be your Realtor, lawyer, lender, home inspector, insurance agent, property manager, contractors, handymen, paralegal, and your accountant. Together, this network is much stronger with their collective wisdom and support than an investor with a couple of 'contacts'.

The path to becoming a successful real estate investor is never full of perfect, euphoric experiences. You might think that if you do all the right things, everything will work out perfectly for you, but problems and obstacles will come up. This is part and parcel of pursuing and achieving ambitious goals and building a better life for you and your family. Pursuing your ambitions and goals can be grueling along the way, but achieving those goals is among life's most gratifying and exhilarating experiences.

Along the investing path you will definitely get thrown a curve ball or two, and it never comes at a convenient time. Repair requests, tenants' disputes, an insect or rodent issue, a tenant paying late, a sudden vacancy; there are a range of issues that could occur.

Knowing it will happen and already having a supportive network around you is a huge step towards getting things taken care of. As you overcome problem by problem, you will naturally gain more knowledge, problem-solving skills, independence, and personal confidence. You will literally feel unstoppable as a property investor, and this newfound confidence and problem-solving abilities will show up in other parts of your life as well.

Most people don't immediately think of their network as a key component to their real estate investment success because they can't peg an immediate ROI (return on investment) to it. If you have big dreams, you'll need big teams. You can't do it all yourself. Having this network behind you from the start literally puts you in a pretty powerful investment position.

Sometimes, things happen at our rental properties that are in other cities, at a more often than not inconvenient time (for example late at night), and in need of quick attention and resolution. On one such occasion, we had a furnace break down at one of our single-family home properties on one of the coldest nights of the year. It was the night before I had to jump on stage and do a presentation for almost 1,000 investors, and I didn't have that presentation ready yet. With one call, I was able to reach out to one of our trusted furnace technicians. He then called the tenant, set up a time to go over that very night, and the problem was fixed. This all took place after 10 pm on a Friday night. I don't know if you've ever needed your furnace replaced after 8 pm on a weekday, never mind 10 pm on a Friday night. Any company would have you waiting until the next morning at best. The ability you have as an investor to make a call, especially after hours, to resolve something that needs immediate attention just goes to show how valuable a strong network can be.

All problems can be solved with the right network, and investing in your network is by far the single best investment you can make. Your network will help you get answers, overcome obstacles, solve problems, better leverage opportunities, and open doors you didn't even know existed. The value of having a strong network where you can quickly reach out and ask, "How should I handle this? Do you know anyone who can fix…? What do I do when…? Your network literally acts as a support group. Calling on your network can save you countless hours of calls, research, money, pain, and sleepless nights. Not knowing the answer or how to deal with a unique situation as a landlord is an unnecessary stress that you don't want or need, but it will happen. You want to be able to get answers quickly and act decisively when a problem arises. There is enormous value in arriving at a decision. It is the failure to arrive at a decision that keeps our mind going in maddening circles as if we are on a hamster wheel. I find half of our worries vanish once we arrive at a clear answer of what the right thing to do is. To minimize worry down to the least amount of time possible, you should accept what needs to be resolved, decide who in your network would best be able to help with a resolution, get the answer, and take immediate action.

Conversely, not having a network or having people in your network who don't specialize in investment real estate might lead to unnecessary stress and potential financial loss. This won't happen in every case, but you are definitely setting yourself up for trouble if you don't use professional advice when making the biggest investment of your life. When something comes up and you don't have a specialized network, are they really going to be able to give you the best advice or steer you in the right direction? One can save a few hundred bucks on the front end by just looking for the cheapest service provider, but it can cost you thousands on the back end. We've all been there. We cheap out on a service or product, and it ends up either leading to disappointment and frustration and/or costing us more in the end.

There is no way we could have gotten any other reputable company to go out and repair the furnace that Friday night. Our guy wasn't the cheapest, but he was also not the most expensive. But because he was part of our network, he went above and beyond, which money can't buy.

The cheapest lawyer or paralegal is probably not going to be one you can call after hours to get a legal question answered that you need an answer for ASAP. The lawyers in our network take our calls even after weekday hours and on weekends. It's not often that we need to make these after-hours calls, but sometimes a situation can't wait, and it is reassuring to know that we have the support to get answers for matters that can't wait until the next business day.

The same principle applies to mortgage brokers and lenders. Different lenders and banks have different qualification requirements for loans, and they will all offer you different terms and deals. While with one bank you might not qualify to purchase a property, with another you might suddenly qualify for a couple of properties. You need a lender who understands how different banks qualify prospective buyers and what their caps are on the amount of properties one can own.

When you have a strong network, you are better able to get repairs or fixes done in emergency situations, getting an honest job done well without paying a fortune. You're able to get financing for more properties than what your own bank could provide to you and not have issues closing on a property. You're able to reach a lawyer or paralegal after hours to get advice on a property or tenant matter. You're able to get answers from fellow investors and your investment Realtor when you need guidance with a problem you've not come across before.

Amazing people know other amazing people. Surround yourself with people who are not only good people, but are also very good at what they do. Once you form that network, cherish it as if it were family. I would argue that your network is next most important to your family. If it wasn't for my network, I know our life would be nowhere near where it is today. With my network, I literally feel I am standing on the shoulders of giants. I am a true believer of the saying, "You are the average of the five people you hang around most." With a powerful network, the seemingly impossible becomes possible, and the power of a strong network can be felt in ways you cannot imagine.

Your real estate investment dream team

Your Realtor

Your investment path usually starts with your real estate sales representative. This is what my team and I have been doing for over 15 + years. Your Realtor should specialize in investment real estate and essentially be the captain of your team. There's a lot more to do than opening the doors to potential listings and making suggestions and phone calls. Desirability of property type and location changes as neighbourhoods change. Rents change, advertising strategies for tenants change, the health of universities and colleges change, and infrastructure in towns and cities change. Nothing is stagnant in real estate; instead everything is dynamic and ever changing. As an investor purchasing a property, you need to know these things, and if you are not personally on top of these changes, you need someone who is. Does your Realtor know bylaws, zoning, contractors, handymen, property management companies, and what you can and can't do with a property? Do they have access to off-market deals and priority access to new releases? They don't necessarily have to have all the credentials noted above, but if they do, you may find working with a person or team with this type of background will make your investment career a heck of a lot easier.

Your Realtor will find, gather, and analyze information of potential listings that fit your criteria. This involves more than just setting a buyer up on an automatic notification system where they are emailed and receive listings within their budget range. Anyone can pretty much do that. This means sifting through each listing looking at the pros and cons of each potential property. It means crunching numbers to see if the potential investment makes sense. It means booking and viewing the properties that make the cut and should be investigated further. It means physically going through properties, or plans for properties if it is a new build, and concluding whether or not the property qualifies as a good investment opportunity or not.

Eventually, after being presented with a few investment properties, you'll discover a property that you can see yourself buying. At that point, your Realtor will write up an offer for you. Although you're the one who ultimately determines how much to offer, the real estate agent is responsible for helping you understand the various sections of an offer and helping you put your offer together. While writing up the offer, the Realtor often inserts clauses on the agreement of purchase and sale to protect the purchaser. The most common clauses provide the option for the purchaser to back out of a deal if needed before firming up. For instance, a financing and inspection clause are two of the most common clauses that are inserted in an agreement of purchase and sale. These clauses give the purchaser the opportunity to walk away from the offer, with no financial loss, in the event that the purchaser doesn't get financing approval for the property or simply doesn't like the results of the property inspection report.

The first offer a buyer puts forward is not usually accepted by the seller. Offers and counteroffers are a very important part of the transaction, as they can save or net you thousands of dollars on a purchase or sale. In the event that the seller is willing to negotiate with you, your agent will negotiate on your behalf. During the transaction, buyers and sellers don't actually communicate with each other directly. Instead, the Realtors representing the buyer and seller will do the communicating so that it all stays above board. Negotiating a purchase or sale of a property is much like being at a poker table. For us investors, a purchase or sale comes down to the numbers. If the numbers don't work, we agree to disagree with the seller or buyer, and we move on. We will let someone else overpay for a property if we don't see the value.

Eventually, you will come to an accepted offer. The Realtor will then facilitate a property inspection and coordinate the deal documents for the mortgage broker or lender and your lawyer. The Realtor will help with a lot of the communication between you, the lender, and the lawyer so that everyone is on the same page when it comes to the details of the offer. Once the investor is satisfied with their purchase and has fulfilled any offer conditions, i.e. financing and inspections, we can move forward and firm up on the property.

When the investor finally takes possession of their investment property, the Realtor will often help the investor to ensure a smooth handoff. If the property is already tenanted, the Realtor will assist with the signing of new leases. If the property is not already tenanted, the Realtor can help the investor to fill their property. If the investor wants to have a completely hands-off investment, we help with getting leases signed or get a property management company involved to fill and manage the property.

Your lender

After your Realtor, the lender you choose will be your next most important team member. The lender is who helps get your deal funded. I, and the majority of investors I work with, have been using one of the top ranked lenders in Canada for the past 20 years. As discussed in Chapter 5, there are other options for financing as well; the big five banks, a credit union, B-lender, or private lender.

The lender's first job is to get you a 'preapproval' that provides you with the details of how much you can afford for a property and how much of a down payment you will need to come up with to put down on the property. Currently, in Ontario, a buyer purchasing a principle residence that they or their family will live in can qualify for the purchase of a property with a 5% down payment for properties $500,000 and less. From $500,000 to $999,999, 5% of the first $500,000 of the purchase price is required and 10% for the portion of the purchase price above $500,000. For a property that is 1 million or more, the down payment requirement is 20% of the purchase price. If the buyer is purchasing a rental property that they or their family are not going to live in, a 20% down payment is typically required. The preapproval will let you know how much you are approved for (how much of a house you can afford) and how much of a down payment you will need to have access to for the purchase. See Chapter 5 on how to get access to a down payment for more information on this process.

Your contractors and handymen

As demonstrated by my earlier furnace example, problems will come up at the most inconvenient times; a leaky dishwasher, a broken fridge, sewage backup, a broken furnace or AC. You're making income, so you are going to deal with problems. However, with the right network these 'problems' are literally saved with a phone call. You want to be at peace in moments of chaos. A strong network of tried and tested contractors and handymen is the most productive way to push forward with maintenance calls. As investors and landlords, we put ourselves in a positional advantage by already going into this with a strong team behind us.

If you don't have access to a network of contractors and handymen, you would need to trust referrals from friends or search for someone online. When choosing a contractor that you haven't used before, you definitely don't want to go with the cheapest quote. Cheap can mean all types of things. The two-day repair can turn into two months. If the work is not done properly you will need to get another contractor to fix the original contractor's work. The contractor could take your money, not complete the job, and disappear. I've seen it all. Luckily, after over 20 years of working in investment real estate, we have gone through our fair share of 'bad' contractors and handymen, but in the last decade the cream has risen to the top. We now have a strong network of contractors and handymen who are not only able to do the odd touch-up and repair on properties for us but have also rescued us in situations where we needed action right away.

Your home inspector

The purpose of a home inspection is to have a qualified home inspector go through and examine your property to establish its condition and raise any concerns before the offer is finalized. Unfortunately, the bar to qualify as a home inspector in Ontario is much too low in my opinion. Presently, the successful completion of a one- or two-week course enables anyone in Ontario to qualify and operate as a home inspector. This simply means that you shouldn't just rely on a Google search or best price when choosing a home inspector. A property is most often our most expensive investment. This is not the time to cheap out. Getting a good, qualified home inspector will often lead to the final conclusion whether or not we go ahead with the purchase of a property based on the results of the inspection.

We work with quite a few home inspectors who have been in the business for decades.

You want a good inspector who is able to discover and identify if there is something about the property that makes it a bad deal. You can then walk away from the deal instead of making the detrimental mistake of moving forward and potentially risking thousands of dollars in unforeseen repairs that a good home inspector would have alerted you to.

Your accountant

There are numerous accounting specialists. An accountant with experience in real estate investment is typically the person you are searching for. The value of an accountant that specializes in real estate is that they know the legal ins and outs of tax law and real estate investing and will save you money on taxes, which means more money in your pocket. With a good, specialized accountant there are many ways to minimize the amount of tax you would owe to the government at the end of the year.

Your lawyer

It should come as no surprise that we like to use our network of lawyers that specialize in real estate transactions. When purchasing a property, the lawyer will review the purchase and sale agreement, ensure there are no claims against the property, arrange title insurance, ensure you have a valid title on completion, complete the mortgage transaction, make sure property taxes are up to date, exchange legal documents with the seller's lawyer, and get the keys for the property couriered from the seller's lawyer to you.

The value of a lawyer whose practice focuses on real estate really becomes important when you are in the middle of a difficult situation such as dealing with a problematic seller or tenant, deal, or some issue with the city and the property. Their expertise can save you from frustration and losing money.

A lawyer should also set up your will so that the money from your investment transfers to your beneficiaries in the event of your passing. A good lawyer will use a secondary will as an investment vehicle so that the beneficiaries' taxes are significantly reduced upon inheritance. There is a whole host of disadvantages to passing without a will. Without a will, you do not have an executor. This means someone must be appointed to act as an administrator of your estate, and this comes at a huge financial cost between courts and lawyers. It's morbid to discuss this topic but unfortunately inevitable.

Your insurance agent

One might think choosing an insurance agent should be a pretty straightforward task. However, if you go to three different insurance agents, you will most likely be offered three different types of coverage. As always, the one with the lowest price may not necessarily be the best option. Lower price can mean inferior coverage, and coverages can vary dramatically. Some carriers may have exclusions on their policies removing important coverages such as sewer backup or basement flooding. You need to verify with the insurance agent to ensure you have the coverage you need, even if that means paying a little more. An extra $50 per year can potentially save you tens of thousands of dollars down the road. Types of items to pay special mind to when getting rental property insurance is coverage for water damage, property damage, loss of rental income, rebuild costs, liability protection, and how the annual fee differs with the different deductible options. Protecting your assets starts with getting the right insurance in place.

Your property management

As a property owner, you have the choice of either managing your properties yourself or hiring a property management company. I find that most property owners will typically manage properties themselves, as long as the property is local and consists of no more than three units. With five units or more, I find that most investors will hire a property management company. More units under one roof means more management.

If the investor decides they would rather have their properties looked after by a property management company, the typical monthly fee is anywhere as low as 4.5% of gross rent up to 12%. The management company will also typically charge between 75% and 100% of one month's rent to find new tenants and lease the property.

My team and I are fortunate to work with several of the top property management companies across Southern Ontario. However, when you are a new investor looking for a property management company and you don't have access to a network like ours, the search can be daunting.

The best way to decide which property management company to choose is to ask them the following questions: What are your fees? What happens if I am not satisfied with your service and I want to break the contract? What is your process for collecting rent? Are the tenants set up on automatic withdrawal, postdated cheques, e-transfer? How do you handle maintenance and repairs? Is there a certain threshold, for example less than $200, where you just have the repair taken care of and then bill the owner or do you just go ahead with repair requests and bill the owner later? Do you mark up the repair bill to cover coordination or is the repair bill the final bill? How often do you inspect the properties? How do you market to tenants and fill properties? What social media platforms do you use? How do you screen tenants? What type of application, references, credit cheque, and background screening do you do?

Keep in mind that property managers typically deal with problems. That is what they are there for. They collect rent and deal with issues. It definitely takes thick skin to be a property manager. Once you find a good one, it's a good idea to send them a gift at Christmas. I can assure you many owners don't do this. If you do, it may help make your property more of a priority on their list if you have a vacancy or repair that needs to be taken care of.

Your paralegal

As a landlord, we do our best to fulfill our responsibilities and provide a safe and habitable dwelling for our tenants. Unfortunately, in some rare cases, a tenant might not live up to their side of the bargain and we may need to pressure them with an eviction or actually evict.

As a landlord, the tenant eviction process is pretty straightforward in Ontario, as discussed in Chapter 6. However, if your schedule simply doesn't allow you to follow through with an eviction, you should hire a paralegal to do it on your behalf.

Paralegals are members in good standing with the Law Society of Ontario. They are licensed and have the authority to represent a property owner in the Small Claims Court and Tenant Board Tribunals. They are incredibly affordable with a much lower fee schedule than a lawyer while still providing effective professional legal representation. They can file applications, serve notices, and attend hearings on your behalf. Hopefully, you never need a paralegal on your real estate investment journey, but if you ever do, a good one is worth their weight in gold.

Conclusion

You might study something, read about it, write about it, teach it and talk about it, but if you are not doing it, you're not a specialist. If you don't have a network, you will be figuring this out on your own soon. There's no need to reinvent the wheel. You won't know if you are getting the best advice, the right price, right terms, and best conditions. However, if you have the right network in place, you will have access to up-to-date, niche information that most real estate investors only dream of having access to.

You will have access to people who are the best at what they do. With the right network of property management companies, contractors, lawyers, and paralegals, you will get what you need when you need it, often outside of business hours. You will be able to make the right, informed decisions quickly because you won't be slowed down by trying to figure things out yourself or getting bad advice. It's all been done before, so profit from the knowledge, experience, and mistakes of others before you. Putting up your own money has a funny way of making you learn quickly. Knowledge and expertise come from doing. Having specialists to consult with for five to 10 minutes can save you countless hours and thousands of dollars' worth of mistakes.

Having a great team behind you is one of the necessities of being a successful real estate investor. The more investment experience your network has and the longer they been doing what they do, the better. Remember, you are only as strong as your weakest link when it comes to a team. If you have a great home inspector, a great lawyer, and a great accountant, but a subpar Realtor, you might've bought the wrong investment, and none of those other people can help you. Or perhaps you have a great Realtor but a poor home inspector, and you bought a property that has a major fault that was missed during the inspection. It's vital that you have specialists in this game. Surrounding yourself with remarkable people lifts you up. The more proactive you are with these great people, the more growth you will see both personally and financially.

Getting the right people in your network doesn't happen by accident. You have to work for it, or you have to find one that already exists, like our network. Your network becomes irreplaceable, and the stronger the talent you bring into your life, the more success you will have.

Most importantly, trust me—you won't realize the true value of your network until you really need it.

CHAPTER 8

Your Marketing System for Good Tenants That Pay and Want To Stay

A man who stops advertising to save money is like a man who stops the clock to save time!

– Henry Ford

As real estate investors, we all want our properties to be filled with ideal tenants quickly; tenants who take good care of our property and pay rent on time. There is no time to be sloppy. Choosing the right tenant is just as important and worth your time as choosing a property to purchase. It takes a little more than a few photos, posting an ad or sign, and choosing a tenant that you get a 'good vibe' from.

As a landlord, you are an investor; yes, absolutely. But more importantly, you are also helping another individual or family by providing a roof over their head. If it were not for landlords offering rental housing, we would have a much larger rental housing crisis right now because there are simply not enough purpose-built rentals in Southern Ontario. In exchange for rent, tenants receive freedom from the costs of owning a home: a down payment, mortgage payment, property tax, insurance, and maintenance and repairs. They have geographical flexibility. They can leave your rental, with proper notice, and relocate or pursue other opportunities elsewhere. This is much less expensive than if they owned the property and had to buy and sell repeatedly. Tenants are ultimately paying rent to transfer these risks to their landlords; the property owners. The value of this risk transfer is real, but if owning an investment property didn't come with such an historical upside and prosperity, investors would definitely find an alternative way to invest their hard-earned money for profit.

As investors, we provide good homes for good people. We are providing an essential need—shelter—for people and families who are renting. This is where your customers (tenants) will spend their hard-earned dollars to put a roof over their and their family's heads. Many firsts and many memories will be made in our rental properties.

The first time you ever rent out your property, it might feel like you are letting your teenager drive your car for the first time. You don't know if the car is going to be returned with scratches, dents, fries on the floor, and an aroma that will most likely take you back to your own teenage years. Just as you can prepare your car and set rules and expectations for a potentially precarious driver, you can set rules and expectations for your property by means of properly advertising, screening, and signing a lease with new tenants.

In general, I feel the majority of people have good intentions. But as a landlord, you must do your due diligence before accepting money, signing a lease, and handing over keys to your property to a new tenant.

When I first started investing in real estate, the only options to advertise a unit or property to tenants was a sign, newspaper ad, bulletin boards, and flyers if you wanted to be extra aggressive. Nowadays, there are many options out there for advertising. In this chapter I will be describing the *most* efficient way, devised from proven strategies and time-tested models that we currently use to advertise our rental properties across Southern Ontario. This method is sure to increase the number of good quality applicants and significantly reduce the time and effort it takes to fill one of your rental properties with great tenants.

In my opinion, if you have the time as a first-time real estate investor and the property is local to you, you should at least try to fill it yourself. You absolutely don't have to, but I find, especially if you are considering using a property management company down the road, that if you have never filled a property you might not know exactly what to expect if someone else is doing it for you. Once you have experience of advertising, screening, and choosing a tenant, you will have a much better idea of what is involved and what to expect. This way, you have a much better idea if something is off with a company that is managing your property. I once worked with investors who reached out to let me know that their management company (which they found and chose, not one I recommended), hadn't been able to get many tenants out to the property and the property was still vacant after several weeks of being available. I checked the most obvious place to list a rental in Southern Ontario, Kijiji. Their property was not listed there; I couldn't find it. I checked the public MLS system. Again, no ad for their property. Through some back and forth phone calls between myself, the investor, and the property management company, we found out that the property management company 'thought' the ad was posted but had somehow forgotten to do it. This is rare, but when dealing with a property management company that may very well have a few hundred homes to manage, something like this can fall through the cracks. The investors followed my advice and fired the property management company. They hired a company that I recommended and have been using for years, and in less than one week, great tenants were found, a leased signed, and the first and last month's rent was collected. These were busy investors and it was their first property. They hadn't filled a property before and were little naïve in handing the property over to a property management company and then turning a blind eye. When it's your first property investment and you are not filling it yourself, you need a referral of a great property management company, and you need to stay on top of that company until they find a great tenant for your property.

If you plan to fill your investment properties yourself, the process will prove to be much easier after you read the next sections on proven strategies that we have been using and updating for over a decade to fill our and our investors' properties with great tenants who stay and pay.

Your customers

If you have never invested in real estate before, you will have probably only ever heard bad tenant stories. Yet, there are millions of good tenant stories to tell. We are wired in a weird way. Most people prefer to complain about their day and a situation that upset them rather than share their most recent positive experiences. People who often share negative stories about being a landlord are most often also people who have never even owned a property. They are conveying a story they heard from a person who knows a person who knows another person. I know thousands of landlords, and although unpleasant situations do come up, all of those landlords are grateful that they are real estate investors and own multiple properties.

One of the greatest gifts of being a property owner is that we get to choose our customer. That's right. In what other line of business do you get to choose your customer? If you don't feel your customer (your tenant) is the best fit for our product (your home), you simply politely decline working with that customer until you find a customer you want to work with. If you are an owner of a good rental property in Southern Ontario, you also experience the good fortune of having a ton of customers literally knocking at your door. What other business can come close to this when opening up their doors without significant expenses in advertising and marketing?

Knowing how to effectively advertise and communicate with your customers is paramount when you are filling your rental properties. Methods that used to work years ago (newspapers, bulletin boards, flyers) has now pretty much become obsolete. We're living in a fast-paced time, and landlords need to constantly uncover better opportunities to attract their customers (tenants).

The rental market, and as a result, the rental customer demographic, is growing and changing substantially. Young adults are staying in their parents' homes longer than ever before. There is a giant wave of renters that is going to hit the market soon (millennials).

Since 2019, we have seen a huge shift in renter caliber, demand, and pricing across Southern Ontario. First, higher property prices and rent prices have far outstripped growth in earnings for individuals and families across Southern Ontario. Individuals and families that were once able to qualify to buy a home are now forced into the rental pool longer, or possibly even permanently, due to the property prices of starter homes and the banks tightening their qualification requirements. Add to this the massive influx of millennials, 7.3 million in Canada, who are coming down the pipeline in need of a roof over their head. Millennials now account for approximately 55% of renters, and this number is rapidly increasing. These are unprecedented numbers. A good portion of millennials are going to personally choose renting over homeownership and having to take care of a home. I strongly believe they are about to be the largest generation of renters in our lifetime. For some millennials, it just won't be a choice but rather circumstances that force them into renting. Many are literally carrying the burden of a mortgage (school loans) without the advantage of owning a home. Some just won't be able to come up with the down payment, and for others homeownership is just too expensive. Others would just rather not make the sacrifice that many homeowners make. They prefer not to live on a shoestring budget. They want to enjoy leisure trips, eating out, entertainment—they choose a renter lifestyle that gives them more flexibility.

Accompanying the millennials is another trend; baby boomers who no longer need to live in a large home that they need to clean, repair and maintain, so they want to downsize.

Many are selling their properties and choosing to rent. Some choose to sell the home they own to tap into the equity, becoming renters of a property that the landlord will now need to maintain. This affords the baby boomers more freedom and comfort to enjoy things they have always wanted to do—travel, go on vacations, spoil grandchildren, and help their children financially.

Filling a property with a tenant can often cause anxiety if an investor hasn't done it before. The following proven strategies and time-tested models will definitely put you in the best position to find that ideal tenant. However, not all ideal tenants who are ideal at the start remain that way. Something can happen in a tenant's life at any point that all of a sudden changes their situation and ability to pay rent. These situations are salvageable, and it's a small price to pay when you are in the investment for the long run. For example, about 10 years ago, I filled one of our single-family homes with what was, at the time, ideal tenants. They were great in the beginning. In fact, they were great for a little over five years; literally no phone calls, and rent was always paid on time each and every month. Then, out of the blue, rent stopped coming in on time and we later found out that the couple had separated and the husband had left the home. The wife could no longer afford to live in our rental. She moved out and left behind some furniture and odds and ends she no longer wanted and didn't need to take. She also took it upon herself to take the appliances that we originally provided with the property when they first moved in. For some investors, this would be the end of their investment career. Not because they would be ruined financially but because of the stress it may cause. Some owners just don't want to deal with these types of minor setbacks. My wife and I always have the big picture in mind. We are in this for the long term. We called up some of our contractors and rented a dumpster bin. Everything was emptied from the house. The carpeting was removed in some areas, painting was done where needed, and we purchased new appliances. When all was said and done, we probably spent roughly $8,000 getting that property rent-ready again. After renting the property out for five years, we had accumulated almost $100,000 of the mortgage paid down from the rental income, we had positive cash flow, and had experienced great appreciation on the property. We still own this property today, and the equity it has realized is now in the hundreds of thousands of dollars. I shared this story with you to demonstrate that yes, we want the best tenants for our properties. But that doesn't mean they will always be that way. Luckily, more often than not, great tenants will remain great. But if one goes sideways on us, it is not the end of the world when you keep your eye on the prize and the bigger picture.

Now let's find out how you can attract your ideal tenants.

Where and how to post ads

Lawn signs

One of the truest, time-tested ways to find tenants for your rentals is by posting a 'For Rent' or 'For Lease' sign on the front yard of the property. This sign can simply have the words 'For Lease' with a phone number that prospective tenants can call. These signs are inexpensive and can be procured from many places—local sign shops or online sites where you can customize your own size, for example vistaprints.ca. We use coroplast (corrugated plastic) for lease signs that are then zip tied to the sign post we are using. Usually, you can order the signpost from the same provider that makes the signs.

Unless your rental property is on a high-volume traffic street, which many are not, there won't be a ton of eyes that see the 'For Lease' sign. If your property is on a quieter street, directional signs with an arrow can be helpful. You can plant these around the neighbourhood to direct people to your property. Compared to other types of advertising, lawn signs will not typically bring in a large quantity of leads, but the leads that do reach out are generally considered good quality leads. These are people who often already live in the neighbourhood. They might already have established roots in the area, such as friends, work, schools for their children, etc. They already know and like the neighbourhood and that is why they are reaching out. Other times, neighbours see the sign and promote our home to their friends or family who might be looking for a property to rent in the area.

Some owners don't feel comfortable posting their cell number on a sign or online ad for everyone to see. There are great solutions for this. Providers like evoice.com and ringcentral.com assign you a cheap virtual telephone number that you can post on signs and online ads. When a prospective tenant calls the virtual number, the owner's voicemail kicks in and the tenant leaves a message. The message can either then be emailed to the investors or sent as a text. During this whole time, the investor doesn't even hear a phone ring. They just get an email voice message or text that they can respond to when they have time.

Kijiji

Kijiji.ca has been the number-one lead source when advertising a property for some time. It's free to post an ad, but there are also paid options if you would like your ad featured as a sponsored ad. Tenants use Kijiji when looking for a place to rent, as it gives them the option to choose the city and area they desire and type of home they wish to rent. You can showcase up to 20 pictures of the property for lease to go along with the ad itself.

We teach investors that we work with how to write and post a great for-lease ad on sites like Kijiji.ca. Before they post their ad, we ask them to send their write-up to us so that we can review and often tweak it, especially if it is their first time writing a lease ad. You never get a second chance to make a good first impression, and you don't want to lose out on a great lead due to a poorly designed ad.

A for-lease ad shouldn't read like 90% of them do; the classic Realtor description: three-bedroom, two-bathroom home, hardwood flooring, oak cabinets, great neighbourhood. The info is there, yes, but the ad itself significantly lacks emotional appeal. When we write ads, we prefer to take our time constructing an ad that gives our prospective renters an idea of what it would feel like to live in our home. We write out a little story about the property, adding such details as family friendly neighbourhood, quiet street, open concept home great for entertaining, lots of natural light, walk out from dining room to back deck, and fully fenced backyard that is great for summertime barbecues with friends and family. Are there grocery stores and other desirable amenities nearby, for example parks, restaurants, Starbucks, Shoppers Drug Mart, churches, recreation centers, etc.? We need to include those. How about public transit; is it convenient and nearby? Does the property have a great walk score? If so, let's mention that. This type of ad gives renters a better idea of what it would be like to live in our properties.

Once our ad is posted, tenants will either respond to it via email or call the number if we leave one. Personally, I like to leave my cell number in the ad to give the tenant options of their preferred method to reach out and set up an appointment to view the property.

Good quality photos

Getting quality photos is probably the easiest thing to do in all of real estate investing, yet somehow 50% of online ads for rental properties have brutal photos. Instead of showcasing the property, they are dark, uninviting, and taken carelessly from weird angles. Any potential tenant is likely to just quickly skip to the next ad. Photos are always what grabs our prospective tenant's interest first. If they like the photo, they will read the ad. A little effort goes a long way here. First, photos of the property need to be seasonally relevant. Too often I see a house listed for lease in the summertime, but the photo shows snow on the ground and trees with no leaves. The same happens in winter, with people posting summer photos with nice green grass and leaves on the tree. The problem with this is that tenants are likely going to wonder whether the landlord has been trying to fill the house for months. An old photo might make it look like the property has been on the market for a whole season, or two, and tenants will think something is wrong with the property.

Paid vs. free ads

Although it is free to post an ad on Kijiji.ca, there are a couple of paid options as well. We ran an A/B split test on Kijiji to figure out what works best for us, a paid ad or the free ad post. To do this, we ran the exact same ad for a rental property; one as a paid top ad and the other as a free ad post. We then kept daily stats on these two ads. Our stats revealed that the paid ad received three times as many leads as the unpaid ad. For now, we've definitely confirmed it pays to pay for a top ad on Kijiji when advertising a home for rent. By paying for top ads, our ads get displayed in two different locations: within the dedicated top ad section of its category as well as its regular unpaid spot in the search results. This helps boost the listing's exposure, and because of the prominent position of the top ads, our listings get the most views and responses.

It is also possible to include a video of the property on Kijiji.ca. A video is a great way to further give prospective renters and idea of what it would feel like to walk through the property. It can be as simple as grabbing your cellphone and recording a video while walking through the property. You can then upload and include the video in your ad.

If you choose to not pay for a top ad when posting on Kijiji.ca, you want to monitor your ad closely. When placing a free ad, your post goes to the top of the free section. When the next user posts their free ad, they bump your ad down a spot on the page. This continues as new ads are added. Kijiji has a limited number of ads per page, usually about 30. Once your ad goes beyond page five, it's pretty much lost in the abyss. That's over 150 ads that a user would need to go through before they get to yours. They are most likely not viewing 150 ads. To make sure your ad is seen, you either want to delete and repost your ad or pay to bump it up. Bumping up your ad pushes your ad back to the start of the queue, to the very first section on the first page of the site. Monitoring what page your ad is on is a must to make sure your ad is actually being seen.

Other similar rental sites we use include zumper.com, padmapper.com, and gottarent.com, but they definitely don't attract as many leads as Kijiji.ca does.

Newspaper

Advertising in the local newspaper is becoming less and less popular among owners when advertising a property for lease. For some reason, newspapers haven't adjusted their expensive pricing to compete with free and cheap online ads. With more eyes on online ads and less on the ad section of a newspaper, we almost never post our properties in the local newspaper. However, I will include the best way to do this just in case your market calls for posting an ad in the local paper.

A newspaper ad should be short and sweet because you typically get charged per word or per line, depending on the paper. The ad should include the area of the property, a brief description of the home and its location, and the number prospective tenants should call if interested. For your ad to stand out, the best thing to do is call the newspaper, talk to someone in the classified section, and ask if they have a special on any ad postings. They don't advertise this. You need to call them. Sometimes the special can include a free photo of your home or some extra lines for free. Take advantage of those upgrades if there is a special. If there are no specials, you can make your ad stand out by choosing what is called reverse print at the top of your ad. Ads are typically black font on a white paper background. Reverse print means the top of your ad is black and the print on it is white. Your ad automatically draws the reader's attention because it stands out. The small fee you pay for this feature is negligible considering the competitive advantage you'll gain over other ads.

Facebook

There are several options when it comes to advertising a rental on Facebook.

Your ad on Facebook will be very similar to an ad on Kijiji. You'll need a title that helps your ad stand out, a description of the property, and decent photos to showcase it.

The volume of responses to ads can be higher on Facebook than on Kijiji, but we find the quality of these leads a little less strong than the leads we get from Kijiji. The major difference between running an ad on Kijiji and Facebook is that prospective tenants using Kijiji were searching for your ad. They specifically went to the rental section of Kijiji and looked for properties available for rent. When a person is on Facebook, they usually don't log in to the site specifically looking for a rental property. They may be posting one of their favorite pics or checking their feeds when they come across your property for rent. They might not even be in the market for a rental property, but your ad caught their attention. The great thing about an ad on Facebook is that there is a much better chance that people will share your post with others they know who might be looking for a rental.

On Facebook, you can also see the profiles of potential tenants who enquire about your property. You can learn a lot from what people post and how they interact with their friends online.

Regardless of whether you post your rental ad on Facebook or not, those social media platforms are useful screening tools to use when you are considering a tenant and doing your due diligence.

With a site like Facebook, you can often confirm if the tenant's employment details match what they listed on the application with just the click of a button. Does your property have new hardwood floors? Are you worried that the tenant might have a large dog? Some of the most popular profile photos on Facebook are family photos with a beloved family pet!

Booking appointments

The purpose of your ads is to get tenants to your property. You are setting up an 'appointment', not an open house, when showing your property. Telling tenants or advertising that you are having an open house is the biggest mistake an investor can make. By setting up an appointment, you are getting a commitment from a family that they are coming out to view your property on a particular date at a particular time. The goal is to get all prospective tenants to your property at the same time. This creates an auction-like environment— it is all about supply and demand. You can't do this if you are telling tenants you are holding an open house on Saturday between 2 pm and 4 pm. First, when saying you are doing an open house, there is no commitment from the tenants to show up. If something comes up on their end or it just happens to be great weather and they want to spend time with their family that day, there is no reason for them to call you and cancel because you said you were doing an open house, which means you would be at the property whether they show up or not. Conversely, if you set up an appointment, people are respectful. People typically show up for appointments, and if something comes up they will usually be respectful and let you know they need to reschedule or cancel. When setting up the appointments, you should give each and every tenant the exact same times to show up, once in the week and once on the weekend, and that is it. For example, if I am calling back a prospective tenant who enquired about the property, the call would go something like this: "Hi it's Mike, I am returning your call about the home we have available for rent located at [wherever the property is located]. Just wondering if you have any questions about this property…." The words, "returning your call" are huge. Remember, they are getting a phone call from a phone number that has never called them before. To lower their guard right away and prove I am friendly and not a teller marketer or some kind of agency, I let them know right away that I am calling them back, not just calling them out of the blue. Most often, the tenant will ask: "Is the property still available?", and "I would like to set up an appointment to see it. When can I come by?" Sometimes they will ask further questions about the home that they couldn't see from the pictures or read in the description, for example "How many parking spaces are there?", or "Is there a fully fenced backyard?", or "Does the home have central air conditioning?", etc.

The goal is to answer those questions followed by, "I can be at the house Saturday at 1 pm, would that be a good time for you to see the home?" As a backup, you should have one weekday time ready as well, for example Wednesday at 6:30 pm. Only having two date and time options is strategic so that we can control our time running out to show the property versus just going out every single time a lead asks to view the property.

If you don't do it this way, it is going to take much longer to fill the property. If you do personal showings, what often happens is the family goes through, they have no idea of the demand we have for the property because they didn't see you show it to any other families. They might say they have some other properties to look at before making a decision. Life gets busy, they drag their heels and don't get back to you or maybe they do get back a few weeks later when you have already filled the property.

When showing a property to tenants at the exact same time others are viewing it, they will see the demand. If they are on the fence about your property, seeing the demand will make them afraid of missing out, thinking that if they don't decide now they might lose the opportunity.

I clearly remember the day this couldn't have become more obvious to me. It was many, many years ago when I was at a car lot looking at a car. I sat down with the salesperson to negotiate the purchase of a car. The car was a two-door silver Acura RSX, standard with black leather, and there was only one like it on the lot. Just before we started negotiating, he told me that a girl had been in earlier looking at that very car and said she would be back with her parents. We went back and forth on negotiations for about 30 minutes. I played it cool, knowing deep down that I wanted to purchase the car, but I also wanted to get the price down as low as I could. I told him I might need to sleep on it. He pointed to the parking lot just behind me through the showroom window and said, "Oh, here comes that girl that was in this morning with her parents." I immediately said, "I'll take it!" It was all about supply and demand. There was one car and one person (me) interested at the time I was at the sales center. There was no auction environment. But as soon as that second buyer came back, there were now two people who were interested but only one car. This is why the auction environment works so well when we are filling properties. More people at the property at the same time leads to a higher number of applications being filled out on the spot. Some investors ask me, "Don't the tenants get upset because they thought they were the only ones coming to see the property?" That's a completely valid question, but don't worry. I've only ever had that kind of a response two or three times out of multiple hundreds of properties that I have filled. If this happens, simply respond, "Some others reached out and I told them I would be at the house this date and time and they showed up." That's the truth. In this business, there should never be any deceit or anything hiding behind the curtains. Life is so much easier if you are honest and upfront with people. No need to come up with some kind of elaborate lie that you have to remember; that's such a waste of energy.

With the auction strategy approach, you are taking control of your time. You got into real estate investing to earn freedom and don't want to have your time consumed by your properties. Here you are taking charge and protecting your most valuable asset: your time.

When setting up showing appointments, it's important to not pre-screen potential tenants over email or while you're talking to them on the phone. By pre-screening at this stage, you might be disqualifying tenants, which means fewer people will show up at the house during the showings, detracting from the auction environment. When you reach out to prospective tenants to book the showing, you might have anywhere between two to 10 leads to get back to each day, depending on the demand for the property. Your calls to the tenants shouldn't be any longer than five minutes max. If you try to pre-screen tenants over the phone, that five-minute phone call can potentially turn into a 15- to

30-minute phone call. Now, if you have to make several phone calls in a day, this will really burn up a lot of your time. Control your time, keep the conversation short, and set up one of the two times and dates available that week for showings, and that's it. Once the tenants show up at the house and fill out an application, you will discover if they are the right fit or not.

The other nice thing about meeting somebody at the house is that while they might not be a great candidate today (perhaps there was something about the house that didn't suit their needs, perhaps their move-in date doesn't work), they are great to have on the Rolodex for the next property you may purchase or already have in the area that may become available in the future.

When scheduling appointments with prospective tenants to view the property, you always want to end the conversation with, "**Will** you please call if you have to cancel?", as opposed to, "Please call if you have to cancel." When you say **will** and they say, "Yes!", you're getting a commitment from them as opposed to issuing a demand.

To ensure a really good turnout at the property, you should call or email the tenants the night before or the day of the appointment just as a reminder. People are busy. That initial appointment you set up with them might have been discussed on a Sunday for a Wednesday showing. Come Wednesday, if you didn't make a follow-up call, they might have simply forgotten about the appointment. By making that reminder call, you will get a higher turnout conversion rate.

Showing your property, getting applications, and tracking leads

The day has come. It's time to show your property. I really personally enjoy this part. You get to meet a lot of people, you're helping out a good family, and you're potentially forming a relationship with a tenant whom you may have in your property for five to 20 years.

As a property owner, your demeanor during these showings should just simply be that of a person helping another person; casual and friendly. You never want to come across as Mr. or Mrs. professional Realtor or salesperson.

It is also essential that your property creates a welcoming first impression. Start with the exterior. Some tenants might not even enter a home if the exterior is not well maintained. Make sure the grass is cut, shrubs are not overgrown, snow is shoveled, and there is no garbage or debris on the lawn, driveway, or steps.

Inside the home, the brighter the better. All lights on. Consistent soft white bulbs in your light fixtures are not necessary, but ideal. They give the home more of a cozy feel versus the bright white LED lights that can give off an energetic or office feel. Have the blinds and curtains open. A bright room looks larger and more inviting. Make sure all toilet seats are down. Appliances, countertops, and mirrors should be clean. You don't have to do any of the cleaning yourself. You can simply hire a handyman to cut grass or shovel snow and a cleaner to give the house a once over if you have limited time. Then simply show up at the property 15 to 20 minutes before the showing to turn on the lights, open the blinds and curtains, and make sure everything is ready.

Once the potential tenants show up, greet them, thank them for coming, ask them to sign a sign-in sheet, and then tell them, "Take a look at the house, if you have any questions I will be in the kitchen." Don't follow them around like Mr. or Mrs. Realtor trying to sell them a property. Let them wander around and get a feel for the house. Once they finish looking around, they will meet you in the kitchen and discuss whether they like the house or not. If they like the house, the next step is for them to fill out a rental application on the spot. You need several rental applications and pens ready at the property. Don't allow the tenants to leave with an application. If one family sees someone leave with an application, they will generally all want to leave with an application. Letting prospective tenants leave with an application is not a good idea for a couple reasons:

First, when the application comes back, it is often hard to put the tenant's name to the face. You met a few people at the property, you heard a few life stories from tenants, what they do for a living, if they are married or not, have children or not, do their kids go to the local school, did they say they have a large dog, were they the ones you saw smoking before they came into the house to meet you? Trying to put a face to the name on an application a day or two later can prove very challenging. Second, they might have no interest in the property but felt the need to ask for an application that they would "send later" as a polite way of leaving the house. In this case, simply respond with, "I have a limited amount of applications here and I need these. If you are interested in the home, feel free to email me and I will gladly send you an application."

Once a tenant has filled out an application on the spot, review the application right then and there. First and foremost, confirm their financial ability to afford rent. As landlord, you want to see that their gross monthly household income is equal to or greater than three times the monthly rent. This should be sufficient enough where they are not scraping by to cover the rent and provide for other necessities. Also look at length of employment. Ideally the application should show long-term employment, implying commitment and stability. If they just started a new job, ask them how long they were with their previous employer and what their reason was for leaving. Did they get fired, quit, did they switch jobs because the new one pays better or has better hours? If you ask, they will tell you. You also need to see how long they have been renting at their present place, how much are they paying, and why they are leaving. Preferably, they would have been renting at their current residence for over a year and have perhaps outgrown that property. Perhaps the landlord is selling or they don't like where they are living. You want to make sure what they were paying in rent at their current rental is not too far off from the rent amount you are asking for your property. For instance, if a tenant is paying $1,200 a month all-inclusive for a one-bedroom apartment and they want to rent your three-bedroom, two-bathroom bungalow for

$2,200 plus utilities, you need to verify this jump in monthly expense is affordable for them.

If at first glance their application shows that their gross monthly household income is equal to or greater than three times the monthly rent, they have good history with the rental they are currently in (they have been in the property a year or longer) and you have a good gut feeling about them, you can ask for a deposit. You are not going to accept this family as your tenants yet because you still have to do your screening. But if their application looks good and you get a good feeling about them, you want to collect a deposit as soon as possible. You simply say, "Your application looks good; would you be willing to put a deposit down so that I can hold this house for you?" Then let them know that you still have to do your credit, employer, and landlord reference check on them and that their deposit will be refunded if you don't select them for the home.

It is important to collect a deposit straight away. Otherwise, what often happens is after you have called their references and run a credit check and you call the prospective tenants back a day or two later, they sometimes just go MIA or say they have found something else. They can easily do this because they have made no commitment.

However, when you collect a deposit, they now have skin in the game. That deposit being 100% refundable if you don't choose them as your tenants.

When you ask for a deposit, the tenant will most likely ask, "How much of a deposit are you looking for?" Your answer should always be, "How much would you be willing to put down?" You don't know if they would be willing to give you $50 or $100 out of pocket or if they are able to provide you with the first and last month's rent. Back in the day, people had to write a cheque or go to a bank machine, but nowadays people are e-transferring the deposit on the spot.

Tenants place a higher value on and have greater appreciation for your property when they have paid a deposit. They immediately feel the product, your property or your unit, is 'theirs'. When a prospective tenant doesn't put down a deposit, they have time to review, debate, go look at other properties, and more often than not, against what is best for them, decide to not move forward with your property. We have never had a tenant cancel when they have put a deposit down and that is a fact!

Once a tenant gives you a deposit, you must provide them with a deposit receipt that explains what the deposit is for, i.e. to hold their prospective position for the property and apply towards their last month's rent, subject to the landlord's final approval.

Tracking leads

When advertising your property for rent, you want to find out what form of advertising is working best for you. To do this, you should have a one-page sign-in sheet that you ask prospective tenants to fill out when they enter. They simply need to write in their name and number and check off how they found out about your property. This way, not only are you able to keep track of who was at the property but also find out what type of advertising is working best. If you are advertising in the newspaper but Kijiji ends up being the main source of your leads, you can ditch the newspaper and double down your advertising on Kijiji. Tracking your leads just gives you the ability to be more efficient with your advertising expenses and attract more people to your properties.

Background checks

You'll most likely find that only about 15% to 20% of tenants who view your property show promise to move on to the next step of qualifying. This is normal. You want to do a good job screening tenants to avoid headaches later on. I want to expand your knowledge and skillset here so that you can best avoid the hassles that some inexperienced landlords face. For those tenants whose applications you review and like, you should quickly move on to background and reference checks to verify that they are in fact a good fit. You want to keep the momentum going here. If these are not the right tenants for your property, it's best to find out quickly so that you can move on to finding your ideal candidate. There is no reason why you shouldn't be getting back to the prospective tenants whose applications you are considering with an answer in less than 48 hours, dependent on how quickly you can get your background and credit checks completed.

Credit check

If an investor ever makes a mistake as a landlord, it is generally right here. You mustn't get lazy when filling your rental properties! Once you have several properties under your belt and have filled your fair share of properties, it can seem 'so easy'! The first time is always the hardest because it is new. The first time an investor fills their rental they always dot their I's and cross their T's. After filling your properties with renters a few times, you start feeling like a pro. A landlord that feels like a pro can sometimes let down their guard if they feel they have a good gut extinct and can read people well. You can't just rely on your gut when filling your rentals. This can come back to bite you. I've seen some of the cleanest, friendliest, wholesome families with a great story, very polite, application looks fantastic, they have cash for a deposit, they've come in to see the property for rent, and are super prepared. Then, after running their credit score, we find out that they are drowning in debt, maxed out on all their credit cards, and have several different collections against them. This is not to say they won't pay our rent, since everyone needs a roof over their head, however, if someone is going to have trouble paying rent, there's a very good chance this is the type of candidate that will prove challenging.

An individual's credit score is impossible to hide, for good or bad. The credit report is evidence of their willingness and ability to pay their credit cards, loans, various bills, and maybe child support. Credit check reporting companies vary in how they report credit scores, but on average, what would be considered decent credit for a tenant would be a score over 600. Above 660 is good; above 780 is excellent.

In some cases, we have had tenants apply for a rental who were new to the county. They have a great job, but they haven't established credit yet. In those cases, we usually try to collect six months to a year of upfront rent payments, as long as everything else checks out on our background search.

Each person over the age of 18 who is working and living in the rental should fill out a credit report. If someone who is working wants to live in the house but refuses to fill out a credit report, that is an immediate red flag. Tenants know a credit check is standard protocol when applying for a rental.

Sites we like to use for credit checks are naborly.com, tenantverification.ca, and renterchecks.com. Sometimes these sites provide free credit reports, other times they charge up to $25 for every tenant whose credit report you request. I know some investors like to charge a tenant an 'application fee' in order to pull their credit. Personally, I am willing to forego that cost so that I can start the relationship off on a good note. One alternative that I will definitely not entertain is when the tenant hands over their credit report that they personally got online. In this day and age, those reports can easily be doctored, and we would have no idea.

Employer verification

With tenants who are employed, you need to verify with their employer that they are in fact still working at their place of business and are gainfully employed. Before calling the tenant's employer, I suggest first Googling the phone and address of the company that the tenant wrote on their application to make sure it is a legitimate company. If there is no search result on Google for the phone number or address of the company that the tenant provided, that might be a red flag.

When talking to the employer or human resources, you should ask questions like: How long has the tenant been working there? Are they on contract, salary, part-time or full-time work? What is their rate of pay? Is there anything the employer would offer up on the character of the prospective tenant? If they had a house for rent, would they lease it to the tenant? In addition to verifying income by calling their employer, you can also ask prospective tenants to provide their two most recent pay stubs.

If the prospective tenant is self-employed, we need to verify what information we can by requesting their previous two years' tax returns as well as their last two or three months' of bank statements.

Calling the previous landlord

Of all the background checks we do on prospective tenants, this is the one I am the most cautious of, and I don't hold the result in as high regard as I do the credit and employer/income check and pay stubs. This is simply because I can never know for certain that the person I am speaking to is really the previous landlord. Usually it is easy enough to get a gut feel if it is in fact the previous landlord, but sometimes I've felt the answers were just a little too scripted and there were longer than usual pauses on some answers that should have been more quick. Sometimes, the number the tenant gives us is that of a friend pretending to be their previous landlord. Other times, it could be a landlord who is overly excited to get rid their tenant so they give them a glowing review. You just don't know for certain, but you still need to make those calls.

Questions to ask the tenant's current landlord (and ideally their previous landlord too) include:

- How much was rent and what was the timeliness of the tenant's rent payment?

- Did the tenant keep up in good standing with the utility payments?

- Were there many nuisance calls or were all calls legitimate concerns?

- Did they have a pet?

- Did they smoke in the house?

- Did they cut the grass and take care of the lawn appropriately?

- Did they get along with the neighbours and did the neighbours get along with them?

- Has the tenant provided proper notice that they will be leaving?

- Would you rent to this tenant again?

Social media

One of the best ways to learn as much about your prospective tenant as possible is by checking social media sites like Twitter, Facebook, Instagram, and whatever the newest and most popular site is. This insight is just more information that will help you make an informed decision. Do they have a large family dog that they forgot to disclose? Are they often complaining and being aggressive with others? Is the room they are always photographed in well taken care of and neat or a complete mess with holes in the wall?

More often than not, a tenant who has passed all the other screening requirements ends up displaying good characteristics on social media too. However, it is always worth it to quickly check. You also never know; it's a small world, and sometimes you might find that the prospective tenant actually has a friend or follower that you know as well, in which case you could lean on that friend for some insight on them.

Before handing over the keys

The final details that you need to take care of prior to handing over the keys to your new tenants are important ones. Once keys are handed over, some people can be a little less motivated to get what you want from them done.

Before you hand over the keys, you have to make sure you have completed these final items: Collect any outstanding money, usually the first month's rent since last month's would have already been collected as the initial deposit. Make sure the money is either collected in cash, bank draft, or sent by e-transfer. If the property is rent plus utilities, verify that utilities have been transferred to the tenant. If the utilities are going to be paid by the tenant, call the utility providers to confirm that they have opened up an account and the bills will be sent to the tenant. The tenant also needs to provide content insurance for the property; make sure you see a copy proving that they are in fact insured. Make sure there is nothing else outstanding, for example a copy of their driver's license, employment letter, Notice of Assessments, or recent paystubs. You should include all these documents in a folder along with a copy of their credit report, rental application, and the lease agreement.

It's also a good idea to conduct a 'final walk-through' or 'pre-delivery inspection' with your new tenant. Conduct this by walking through the house with them, checklist in hand, making any notes of the condition of the home and how you are handing it over to them. You should also replace batteries in the smoke and carbon monoxide detectors and test them with the tenant present. Have them initial and sign the document as an acknowledgment of doing the walk-through, and document any current issues that they can live with or want to have fixed.

Every time you have a new tenant moving into one of your properties, you must take photos and/or video of the property, inside and out, to document the condition of the property we are handing over.

When filling a property for the first time, all this might seem like a lot to remember. If you have a single-page document listing the items that need to be completed, you'll be less likely to miss something. It's so easy to forget to have the tenant sign something while you're chatting at the property, so be sure to check off every item.

Most importantly, have patience when filling a property. There's no need to panic and rush to get a tenant into the property. Make sure you do your due diligence properly. Making a mortgage payment is not the end of the world. However, having to deal with a disaster tenant can feel like it and can be much more expensive.

CHAPTER 9

What I Wish Someone Told Me When I Was Younger

Tough choices easy life, easy choices tough life

— Jerzy Gregorek

I want investment properties in my life because it provides me with the freedom to spend more time and do more with my family. It allows me to set my children up for their future and also help my children's children with their future. I wanted freedom of choice. The freedom to do what I want to do, when I want to do it. I also wanted the ability to assist family in need and to support organizations with great causes.

You should think about what your goal with real estate is. It will not only help you in making decisions and taking action, but will also help you get through the tough times when things go wrong.

Investing in real estate in Southern Ontario can change your life. You can achieve multiple streams of income, greater wealth, and more freedom than you ever dreamed possible. But it is going to take time. It will not be the result of being lucky; being at the right place at the right time. It will be the result of your motivation, your knowledge, your patience, and your network.

While growing up, I think I, like many people, thought the answer to a good life was to go to school, get a good job, work hard, save, and invest in mutual funds or stocks. I tried all of that in that order, and I wouldn't be where I am today if I kept following that advice. I would be absolutely miserable, struggling to get ahead, and would definitely not have the freedom of choice to do and experience the things my family and I do today. Entrepreneurs, business owners, and investors are the people who are getting wealthier and wealthier. None of this is a result of anything learned in school or university. Employees, the people working for money, are noticing they can afford less and less as income fails to keep up with the cost of living. The system is 100% rigged against the average hard-working Canadian with a job.

I am an average person who has made myself and my clients multiple millions of dollars through investing in rental properties. Everything that is big started small. In the beginning, most people might feel it's not worth the time, money, and effort to make a couple hundred bucks a month of positive cash flow off their first investment property. You must look at the future. The turtle wins the race here. There is no get-rich-quick in real estate despite what you may see on TV. As equity grows in your investment properties, you'll have more money to reinvest and build more wealth.

At first, people might call you crazy. "Tenants are a nightmare", they'll say. "You are going to lose money; the market will go down." Years will fly by, and then they will say you were lucky; you timed the market right. No one is going to say you busted your ass and made your way to success through hard work and sacrifice.

When I first meet investors, many often tell me, "I wish I started investing in real estate earlier, when I was younger." What they don't realize is that every successful real estate investor had to start at some point. I had people telling me 20 years ago they wished they started buying properties earlier, and the same 10 years ago, yesterday, and I will hear it again tomorrow and for the next 10+ years as I continue to work with investors. The only other time better than yesterday is today.

You may think that because I have my real estate license I have selfish motivations to depict how great real estate is. This can't be further from the truth. The real estate market will adjust down. After it adjusts down, it will adjust back up again. The real estate market is cyclical. I don't have a crystal ball so I can't predict when the market will go down. However, when starter home properties do take a dip, I can assure you I will be right there looking for more properties to purchase.

When we start working together, I always ask a first-time real estate investor, "Why do you want to invest in real estate?" The WHY is SO important. The WHY, coupled with their short-term objectives and long-term goals is going to help them realize, experience, and emotionally feel the bigger picture.

The most common answers I hear to peoples WHYs (in addition to any materialistic item they may want to purchase) are:

- I hate my job and want to leave it someday

- I don't get paid enough and I need additional income

- I have no savings for retirement, and I need help

- I want my spouse to leave work

- I want to spend more time with my husband/wife, my children, my family, my friends

- I want to travel more

- I want to attend my child's sporting events/dance recitals/plays, and see them do that thing they will do for the first time, i.e. walk/talk/ride a bike/perform in front of the school/ get an award

- I need to provide shelter and security for my family

- I need to pay for my kids' education

- I want more time to work out, take a course, do yoga, or take up a hobby

- I want more FREEDOM

Through my experience you can have all the above and more and get there a heck of a lot easier by owning assets like real estate.

CHAPTER 10

Getting Started

Don't let your learning lead to knowledge, let your learning lead to action!

- Jim Rohn

The Mike Desormeaux team fosters long-term relationships built on trust and integrity. Our team is responsible for sourcing and identifying suitable real estate and related investment opportunities across Southern Ontario.

We evaluate and structure real estate deals as well as conduct financial analysis and yield projections so that you, the investor, know what you are getting into before you purchase your first investment property.

On any given day, there are thousands of properties listed for sale across Southern Ontario. Choosing the right property, at the right price, in the right neighbourhood, just to start, is paramount when you are investing in real estate.

My team and I are real estate investors ourselves, and we practice what we preach.

We have helped investors purchase over $350 million dollars' worth of investment real estate across Southern Ontario spanning cities including Barrie, Orillia, Pickering, Ajax, Whitby, Bowmanville, Courtice, Oshawa, Belleville, Toronto, Burlington, Mississauga, Brampton, Oakville, Orangeville, Waterdown, Milton, Hamilton, St. Catharines, Vineland, Smithville, Grimsby, Beamsville, Niagara Falls, Brantford, London, Cambridge, Kitchener, Waterloo, Guelph, Georgetown, Woodstock, St. Thomas, and Windsor.

We offer our community of investors a variety of services under one roof, including sourcing and identifying suitable real estate and related investment opportunities, financial analyses on properties, property management, mortgage brokers and lenders, home inspectors, lawyers and paralegals, accountants, contractors, architects, and handymen. Your investment property purchase can be as hands-on or as hands-off as you like.

Whether an investor is looking for a single-family home investment, a duplex, triplex, multi-unit, student rental, property conversion, lot severance and build, or flip, we have their back.

Since we have filled and helped fill over a thousand types of various rental properties across Southern Ontario, we are one of the few teams in Canada that know what rents can be achieved for which properties, roughly how many days a property will take to fill, the best ways to market and advertise a property, and who you can expect to get as a tenant. Keep in mind that government agencies and other tracking systems track apartment rents, not single-family home rentals, student rentals, and second suite property rentals. Most often, property management companies, owners, or teams like us are filling these properties. We are in the trenches on the front line as investors ourselves, and we know our numbers and the market. This knowledge comes from doing the work, and is not information easily accessible to the general public.

My team and I mentor real estate investors on a daily basis, helping them find investment opportunities. We also assist in filling the properties with tenants and providing property management solutions if needed. We a have a strong, trusted Rolodex of all the possible trades you can think of related to real estate investing, ensuring that our investors can spend as little time as they like on this particular asset class. It has taken us thousands of properties and hundreds of contractors to nail down these benefits.

The major benefit of working with our team is that we replace the need for years of experience. You get to reap the benefits, knowledge, network connections, and experience of the successes of hundreds of others without trying blaze this path yourself and making mistakes along the way. You get to build on others' successes, and this model accelerates your real estate investment path.

Ultimately, we all want to be happy. Whether someone is a nurse, a teacher, a parent, a handyman, a financial trader on Bay St., or any of the other thousand things one can do to make a living, the common denominator is we all just want to be happy. Happiness is definitely not measured by how much money we have in our bank account or our net worth. This book has never really been just about money. If it were just about money, I would have never been motivated enough to write this book to begin with. This book was written to help individuals create an extraordinary life.

Whether you are a roofer, salesman, firefighter, or business owner, I hope that a new confidence will take hold of you when you take the first step forward. That first step should consist of reaching out to someone like myself to set up a plan of action to build a portfolio of investment properties. It takes time, but you will be surprised by what just one property can do for your finances and your life over time.

I hope I have expanded and deepened your knowledge of the value and strategies of investing in real estate. I hope this knowledge will be one of the building blocks to helping you experience more of the abundance you can create for your life and the quality of those lives around you. The strategies are not everything, but they should act as a solid foundation to get you going and implementing. Start small, make progress, and before you know it, your goal of financial freedom will be realized. Make sure the people guiding you have your best interests in mind.

I look forward to someday, hopefully, hearing about your success. Perhaps we cross paths and work together.

I want to leave with you the wish that your life be filled with abundance. Abundance in wealth, health, psychology, and relationships. I wish you a life of great opportunity, joy, happiness, and giving. Now go get it!

Sincerely
Mike Desormeaux

P.S. If you are ready, I recommend that you write a note to yourself or even email me explaining your goals with investment real estate, why you want to do it, and what your life will look like once you achieve your short-term objectives and long-term goals. You can share that with me by sending your email to myrealestategoals@wealthwontwait.com I'd be highly inspired to read your goals, why you made them, and the outcome you look forward to. By writing down your goals, I truly feel that somehow, subconsciously, they crystalize in our memory bank. You may not remember them, but one day when you look back, you might find that you've achieved them.

Mike Desormeaux is a licensed real estate sales representative in Ontario, Canada. He lives in Oakville Ontario with his wife and two children.

Mike has spent decades investing in real estate across Ontario. In the process he has helped thousands of investors successfully do the same. You will be hard pressed to find another person in Canada so deeply involved in investment real estate in Southern Ontario.

www.wealthwontwait.com

ISBN 978-1-7773931-0-6

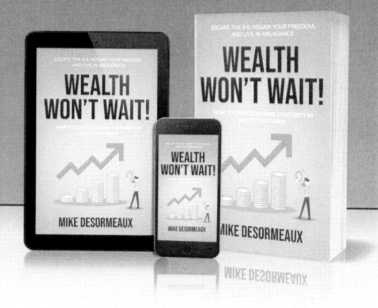

READ THIS FIRST

Just to say thanks for reading my book, I would like to give
you the audiobook version PLUS the accompanying toolkit absolutely FREE.

Go to www.WealthWontWait.com
to register your book

Manufactured by Amazon.ca
Acheson, AB

12265121R00116